"This will give first responders a vivid picture of the care done after leaving the scene and a better understanding of all that goes into being a chaplain. I think it will be reassuring to firefighters to know that when they must rush off to the hospital or the next call, those left behind are being cared for with deep compassion and attention to their needs."
—LESLIE HYNES, communications director, South County Fire

"This book is an invitation to transformation. With Jim Hopper, you will journey into the heart of compassion to discover what it means to be called alongside to help. Read it and imagine yourself making a difference that requires humility, courage, and the presence of the Holy Spirit. We meet those in need beyond the sirens, with all of us held in the loving hands of God."
—MARTY FOLSOM, executive director, Pacific Association for Theological Studies

"Freeze, walk away, or step in? Jim has long been a friend and mentor who makes the choice again and again to step into discomfort and offer his presence. This book is a gift and, as with Jim's life, will buoy courage in your heart to step into the messiness of real life to walk alongside others with love."
—JAMES JOHNSON, pastor, Crossroads Church, Thornton, Colorado

"Having served forty-four years in the fire service, I appreciate the crucial role of chaplaincy. Packed with compelling stories, this book reveals the emotions and thought processes chaplains navigate on each call. A chaplain is an invaluable resource, enhancing the support system for first responders and ensuring better outcomes for the communities they serve."
—TIM SEARS, Director of First Responders, Stronger Families

"Jim Hopper, a fire and police chaplain, shares deeply moving stories about the power of presence when words fail. With gentle candor, he reveals the joys and painful privilege of offering care to victims, families, and first responders during tragic events."
—RALPH FRY, founder and board member, Northwest Incident Support, Hope Unlimited

Beyond the Sirens

Beyond the Sirens

Faith, Compassion the Chaplain's Path

JIM HOPPER

Foreword by Dale Schlack

WIPF & STOCK · Eugene, Oregon

BEYOND THE SIRENS
Faith, Compassion the Chaplain's Path

Copyright © 2024 Jim Hopper. All rights reserved. Except for brief quotations in critical publications or reviews, no part of this book may be reproduced in any manner without prior written permission from the publisher. Write: Permissions, Wipf and Stock Publishers, 199 W. 8th Ave., Suite 3, Eugene, OR 97401.

Wipf & Stock
An Imprint of Wipf and Stock Publishers
199 W. 8th Ave., Suite 3
Eugene, OR 97401

www.wipfandstock.com

PAPERBACK ISBN: 979-8-3852-3144-7
HARDCOVER ISBN: 979-8-3852-3145-4
EBOOK ISBN: 979-8-3852-3146-1

VERSION NUMBER 120924

Scripture quotations marked (ERV) are from the HOLY BIBLE: EASY-TO-READ VERSION ©2014 by Bible League International. Used by permission.

Scripture quotations marked (ESV) are from The ESV® Bible (The Holy Bible, English Standard Version®), © 2001 by Crossway, a publishing ministry of Good News Publishers. Used by permission. All rights reserved.

Scripture quotations marked (NIV) are taken from the Holy Bible, New International Version®, NIV®. Copyright © 1973, 1978, 1984, 2011 by Biblica, Inc.™ Used by permission of Zondervan. All rights reserved worldwide.

Scripture quotations marked (NLT) are taken from the Holy Bible, New Living Translation, copyright ©1996, 2004, 2015 by Tyndale House Foundation. Used by permission of Tyndale House Publishers, Carol Stream, Illinois 60188. All rights reserved.

To my cherished wife, Judy, whose unwavering support and love have been my foundation through every challenge.

And to Mark Warawa, a member of the Parliament of Canada, whose encouragement and belief in these stories made this book possible. Thank you for inspiring me to fulfill my promise.

Contents

Images | xi
Foreword | xiii
Preface | xv
Acknowledgments | xvii
Abbreviations | xix

CHAPTER 1: The Eyes of Despair | 1
This chapter reveals the overwhelming challenges and raw emotions faced by first responders. It highlights the essential role of compassion and faith in providing comfort to those experiencing traumatic loss and showcases what being guided by the Holy Spirit can look like.

CHAPTER 2: What If the Incredible Hulk Was There When You Responded and He Was Really, Really Mad? | 7
Unveiling chaplains' challenges and profound responsibilities as they provide spiritual and emotional support. This chapter explores how the Holy Spirit helps chaplains connect with the families they serve, with answers to prayers arriving at crucial moments.

CHAPTER 3: Where's Waldo? | 18
A familiar face emerges from the crowd, bearing a look of sorrow that hints at an unfolding story. This chapter delves into the healing power of memories and the hidden treasures that emerge when the heart unlocks those experiences.

CHAPTER 4: Held Hostage by Insomnia | 27
Throughout my journey as a chaplain, I've received help in surprising ways. This chapter recounts a remarkable instance of uncanny timing, where a TV broadcast provided invaluable insights just hours before an urgent call, illustrating the Holy Spirit's guidance.

CHAPTER 5: The Heaviest Burden I Carried: Twelve Pounds, Three Ounces | 35

This chapter chronicles the physical and emotional weight of a grieving parent's loss. Through delicate interactions, the chaplain navigates the complexities of grief, highlighting its profound impact on everyone involved, including first responders.

CHAPTER 6: It Depends | 44

This heartwarming event spanned over three years and blessed me deeply.

CHAPTER 7: When Life Unravels | 52

People universally acknowledge some events for the extreme stress they cause, such as purchasing a home, having nowhere to live, death, and marriage. Imagine these not merely as singular events but as a simultaneous surge of a life-altering storm.

CHAPTER 8: How Could a Used Paperback Novel Change a Child's Life? | 62

Help has often come to me in the most unexpected of ways. The likelihood of recalling a tattered, long-forgotten mystery novel I stumbled upon in a state park a decade ago seemed almost astronomical.

CHAPTER 9: Forever Young: Taylor's Legacy | 70

Although we knew nothing about the young girl, we both felt the pressing need not to let her passing go unnoticed. But how do you honor someone you have never met?

CHAPTER 10: Under the Shadow of Wings and a Flag: A Testament of Hope | 84

A frightened bird was able to start a conversation about eternity. It offered a pathway for me to impart hope and comfort. I learned later this was no ordinary bird.

CHAPTER 11: Praise You in This Storm | 95

Amidst the backdrop of overlapping conversations, something extraordinary captured my attention. Talia's twelve-year-old niece began to sing only to herself at the volume of just a whisper. Scarcely audible through the surrounding noise, her whispering caught my attention despite all the other conversations.

CHAPTER 12: Where the Blacktop Ends | 102

In the weary world of first responders, the well of empathy for victims of fentanyl seems to have run dry. "They brought this upon themselves," a common refrain echoes, mirroring a sentiment that even extends to the families.

CHAPTER 13: What Was I Missing? | 111

This chapter explores the moment I understood that sometimes, the lessons we need the most may come from the silence that follows the storm.

Contents

CHAPTER 14: I'm Fine, Really I'm Fine, Thanks for Asking—PTSD | 121

When the sirens fade and the world returns to its steady hum, a different battle often begins in the quiet aftermath of chaotic events. This chapter delves into the silent world of PTSD—a journey marked by unseen scars.

CHAPTER 15: What Would You Say or Do? | 130

Our chaplain group's routine meetings to debrief proved to be immensely beneficial for training. This approach offered a way to accumulate experience without being on the call. Here are some real-life events for your reflection. What would you do?

CHAPTER 16: Teen Suicide Prevention | 140

This chapter stands apart from the others in its purpose and urgency. While much of my work as a chaplain has been about responding to tragedy, this presentation is about prevention—stepping in before the unthinkable happens. Teen suicide is not just a statistic or an abstract issue; it's a devastating reality that leaves families shattered and communities grieving.

Appendix: How Children Grieve | 155

Navajo Way of Listening | 157

LifeWalk Progression Table | 159

Images

All images are mine.

Figure 01. American goldfinch, the state bird of Washington | 88

Figure 02. Recovered by the National Guard searchers | 121

Figure 03. Two-story red wagon at Spokane's Riverfront Park | 128

Figure 04. Doll | 131

Foreword

A CLOSE FRIEND CALLS to tell you that their twenty-two-year-old child has just taken their own life. They want you to come and be with them. As you drive, you wonder: What can I say? What am I going to do? How can I help?

You find yourself in the emergency room alongside the wife of a neighbor. Her husband is six feet, four inches tall and has the physique of an NFL linebacker. He's pacing the hallways of the ER, clenching and unclenching his fists. His anger has everyone on alert. Their seven-month-old son just died. Several police officers and firefighters are standing by, unsure what this distraught father will do. The wife pleads with you to please help her husband.

Situations like this are not uncommon in the lives of police and fire chaplains—called upon at all hours to intervene and care for people who have just lost loved ones or lost their homes and possessions in a fire, or to notify a family of the death of a son or daughter.

Jim Hopper is a chaplain who has been walking into volatile situations for ten years. He shares how God guided him as he cared for individuals and families who were navigating the pain and uncertainty of traumatic events.

I first met Jim and his wife, Judy, at our church. I quickly noticed how naturally they came alongside families and individuals going through some of the most challenging moments of their lives. They offered support with such grace and effectiveness. I was the chaplain for our local police department and worked with other police and fire chaplains covering the southern part of our county. We needed more chaplains, and Jim immediately came to mind. He had an obvious gift for caring for others.

Though Jim and Judy were full-time local real estate brokers, I wondered if he might be interested in chaplaincy. After completing his training,

Jim joined our team as a chaplain with the local fire district and extended his support to law enforcement agencies.

The chaplains in our group came from diverse backgrounds, each bringing their own experiences and personal approaches to the events they encountered. As we met to discuss our calls, it became clear that Jim was uniquely gifted. He had remarkable creativity in the ways he provided care for individuals and families in crisis.

In the stories Jim shares, readers will find powerful examples of how God worked through him to bring comfort in some of the most complex and intense situations imaginable. No amount of preparation can fully equip us for the unpredictable and unique challenges of life's traumatic events. Still, Jim's stories show how faith, compassion, and presence can make a profound difference.

Whether we are chaplains, pastors, neighbors, or friends, we all may find ourselves asking the same questions when we care for others amid trauma: What am I going to say? What am I going to do? Serving as a police chaplain for thirty-one years, I asked those questions en route to every call (usually as a prayer!). While I may not possess the same gifts and creativity as Jim Hopper, I've gained valuable insights from the stories he shares in this book. His experiences have deepened my understanding of how I can better support others during their most difficult moments.

I strongly recommend this book to chaplains, pastors, new and experienced first responders, and anyone tasked with offering support in life's most challenging and chaotic moments.

In closing, I want to acknowledge the incredible team we had the privilege to serve with in South Snohomish County, Washington—some of the most compassionate, capable, and professional law enforcement officers, firefighters, medics, 911 dispatchers, and medical examiner investigators you will find anywhere.

Dale Schlack
Retired Police Chaplain
September 2024

Preface

THIS BOOK IS BORN from my journey as a chaplain serving alongside first responders in some of the most difficult and defining moments of life. Over the years, I've had the privilege—and the responsibility—of standing with people when their world turned upside down. Each call has been a reminder of the fragile nature of life and the resilience of the human spirit. Through countless encounters, I've seen the full spectrum of emotion: grief, fear, hope, and the unexpected strength that emerges when everything feels lost.

This book isn't just about the calls or the work of a chaplain. It's about the quiet lessons I've learned in the spaces between tragedy and hope. It's about the grace and wisdom that often arrive when I've felt most inadequate. More than anything, it's about how these moments have shaped me—not as someone who has all the answers, but as someone willing to step into the unknown and trust that each experience has something to teach.

When I began responding to emergencies, I often questioned whether I would have the right words or enough compassion to help. But over time I realized that the most important thing I could offer wasn't my wisdom or ability, but simply my presence. Being there—fully present—allowed me to witness something greater than myself at work, whether offering comfort to the grieving or finding the right words when there seemed to be none.

I wrote this book to share a few of the stories that have shaped me. Also to invite you, the reader, to see that there is always something more involved, even in the intense moments. I hope that within these pages, you'll find a deeper understanding of the human experience—where faith, doubt, sorrow, and hope often exist side by side. I don't pretend to have all the answers, but I've learned that even amid uncertainty, there is still a sense of purpose guiding us.

Whether you are here to reflect on your experiences or simply curious about what chaplains do, I hope you leave these pages with a sense of connection—to others, to life, and perhaps to something more significant than all of us.

Acknowledgments

HEARTFELT THANKS TO MARTY Folsom whose unwavering guidance has been a constant source of wisdom and encouragement throughout this journey.

To the firefighters of Snohomish Fire District 1: Your dedication to protecting lives and serving our community is truly inspiring. I've had the privilege of standing beside you in some of the most challenging moments, continually amazed by your dedication, compassion, and skills.

Your work goes far beyond fighting fires—you bring hope and comfort to people in their darkest hours. Thank you for welcoming me into your ranks and trusting me to support you and those we serve. This book reflects our shared experiences, and I am forever grateful for the lessons and friendships that have grown from our time together.

To the brave men and women of law enforcement: I extend my heartfelt gratitude to the dedicated members of law enforcement who serve our communities with courage and commitment. Often unnoticed, your sacrifice and strength in the face of life's intense moments have left a lasting impact on me.

Walking alongside you and witnessing your professionalism and compassion has been an honor. Thank you for allowing me to be part of your journey and trusting me during times of crisis. This book is a tribute to your work and to the events we've responded to together.

To the chaplains and volunteers of Support 7, who were always willing to step away from their jobs at a moment's notice to be available twenty-four hours a day to serve others.

Thanks to those special friends who provided helpful suggestions and encouragement in reading my work.

Abbreviations

BC   Battalion chief
ME   Medical examiner
PTSD   Post-Traumatic Stress Disorder

Pager codes:
- F   Female
- FP   Family present
- M   Male
- OD   Overdose
- S   Suicide
- UA   Unattended; no physician present

CHAPTER 1

The Eyes of Despair

Praise be to the God and Father of our Lord Jesus Christ. He is the Father who is full of mercy, the God of all comfort. He comforts us every time we have trouble so that when others have trouble, we can comfort them with the same comfort God gives us.

—2 Cor 1:3–4 ERV

THE EYES OF DESPAIR hold an intense language of their own. As a chaplain, I've learned to speak it fluently, translating the silent pleas and the inexpressible pain etched into the depths of weary gazes.

A heavy antiseptic scent filled the air this day, intensifying the silence. The contrast between the beeping machines and the frail figure in the bed was striking. The family's faces displayed worry, fatigue, and determination as they stood along the wall outside the patient's room.

Reentering the room, the responsibilities and challenges of my role as a chaplain weighed heavily on my shoulders. Lingering doubts about my capability fueled a sense of apprehension that was hard to shake off. As I took those few steps closer, I held a silent prayer in my heart, hoping it would bridge the gap between my uncertainties and the purpose of my presence. When our eyes met again, I earnestly hoped the message was clear—that I cared deeply and was there to offer support, regardless of how daunting the path ahead seemed.

Tears welled in their eyes, each drop a testament to the turmoil they were experiencing. The room, previously buzzing with the undercurrents of frantic activity, fell into a hush. In their gaze, I saw an entire spectrum of human emotion—fear mingled with sorrow, a tinge of regret shadowed by anger. It was a silent call for empathy, a plea for understanding with no words, an invitation to share in a moment of raw vulnerability.

The family didn't belong inside the room while doctors and nurses desperately attempted to stabilize the husband and father. The confined space, already crowded with the medical team, didn't want any extra distractions during their life-saving efforts. They were losing him. His wife shouldn't be a witness to the rough handling necessary to have any chance of saving him. The doctor shouted to keep the wife and family out without looking up. The tone of my response even surprised me as I yelled back, NO! My forceful reply surprised the doctor, causing everyone to look up. Until then, they had concentrated on their tasks and did not notice me standing beside his wife. The doctor's eyes, confused, peered at me over his mask.

Forcefully I explained she had already lost him once today, and it would help her if she held his hand. They understood, creating a space for her to stand next to Joe. Less than five minutes later a single tone filled the room while she held onto his left hand with the wedding ring.

An Hour Earlier

My pager read:

- M 71
- CPR
- Address

After arriving at their home, I reported to the officer in charge. While leading me to the wife, the captain explained they could not stabilize him, and he had coded again. We found June sitting on the bed in the guest bedroom on the main floor. When the medics[1] first arrived and started working on her husband, Joe, they escorted June to this guest room on the

---

1. Sometimes firefighters respond with medics on a call, and I may use either of those terms to describe the personnel on the scene.

main floor. However, she could still hear the life-saving efforts happening to her husband upstairs.

The captain told her what he had shared with me. He explained to June that the medics could not stabilize him and the doctor online from the hospital told them to stop and disconnect the life-sustaining equipment, including the ventilator. She could see him as soon as they finished packing their gear.

Looking around this guest bedroom and seeing a picture of Jesus, I asked if she would like me to pray with her. When June nodded, I felt compelled to ask how she would want me to pray. She responded she would like them to take him to the hospital to give him at least a chance. Holding her hand, that is what I prayed for. As my prayer was ending, the home shook. It was the captain's rapid descent down the stairs. He gave the update that Joe started breathing on his own when they disconnected him. They were going to transport him to the hospital.

June went to find her keys, but I asked if she would allow me to take her to the hospital so she could call her kids during the drive and have them meet us there.

Following behind the medical unit, we discussed concerns about Joe's unstable condition. Acknowledging that information, she shared regretting not being there to hold his hand when the firefighters were upstairs with him. Perhaps this time it will be different, she hoped.

Later, as the quiet of the evening settled around us, I remained with June and her family, a silent guardian amidst their grief. The world outside faded away, leaving only the warmth of their memories to light the room. During these tender hours, while we waited for the funeral home, they granted me a rare glimpse into their lives together. Seeing her smile with her entire face as she spoke delighted me.

As June shared her unexpected meeting story, everyone realized it was a divine appointment. It was clear from her smile, even through tears, that this was the moment she knew he was the one. They were in the third grade.

The stories flowed, each one a cherished memory. They told of adventures big and small, from road trips without a destination to quiet mornings enjoying coffee and the newspaper. One of their favorite tales was about a family camping trip that went hilariously awry when they discovered they had packed everything but the tent. It was a testament to his spirit, always finding joy and wonder in the unexpected, turning every moment into an opportunity for laughter and love.

Now more composed, their children talked about how he could turn a mundane afternoon into an adventure and his uncanny ability to fix broken toys and bruised hearts.

His legacy made a powerful impression on me when I listened to June and her children. Though no longer present in his earth suit, it was a touching reminder of the indelible mark we leave on the hearts of others.

As the evening waned and the funeral home arrived, the stories shared were more than just memories. They were giving the family a jump start on the journey through grief toward the light of remembrance and healing. In sharing their stories, they honored his memory and found comfort in knowing that memories remain.

Throughout this time, I remained silent after simply asking how they met.

Standing in that quiet room, I faced my limitations head on. I realized I couldn't fix everything or make all the pain vanish. It wasn't about having all the correct answers or saying perfect things; it was about being there, fully present for someone in their pain. Listening became my gift, a way to honor their story without rushing.

Then, June's son approached me, eager to share a personal insight that underscored the significance of my role that day. We moved aside for a moment of privacy, allowing John to share his thoughts in a whisper. He revealed how deeply meaningful my gesture of letting June hold Joe's hand was, a detail I hadn't known the weight of. Throughout childhood, people often teased him about his parents' affectionate habit of holding hands wherever they went. Curious, he once asked his mother about it. He never felt the need to ask again after her heartfelt response. June had told him they had been inseparable, hand in hand, since grade school. For her, it was more than a gesture of love: it symbolized safety and unity, making the two of them one. This revelation from John brought an additional layer of understanding to the comfort and connection I had facilitated for June today.

As I reflected, trusting in the gentle guidance of the Holy Spirit, a sense of peace surrounded me. It was like a reassurance that healing could start in the quiet moments between words. That day, I understood my calling. It wasn't about overcoming my limits alone; it was about letting the Holy Spirit use my presence to bring comfort and hope to others.

Standing alongside someone during a moment of profound transformation is a rare privilege few have the honor to experience. Witnessing the Holy Spirit's work in such instances is awe inspiring. At first, I fought the instinct to take action, trying to fix the grief and ease the sting of loss. Quickly, I realized that the depth of my role extends far beyond the immediate impulse to solve problems.

Insights

Navigating the complexities of human emotions during life-altering events has taught me invaluable lessons that have enriched my understanding and approach to life and my calling as a chaplain. Here are some positive takeaways from my experiences:

- Listening as an act of love: Listening has emerged as one of the most powerful tools in my pastoral-care arsenal. Hearing someone's story without judgment or the rush to respond has taught me the true meaning of empathy. It has shown me how listening can be an act of love, offering solace and understanding when words fall short.
- The strength in vulnerability: Witnessing the vulnerability of those grappling with profound loss or change has been a humbling experience. It has taught me that there is immense strength in vulnerability, a sign of courage that inspires and fosters more profound connections with others. It has encouraged me to embrace my vulnerabilities, understanding that they do not diminish my ability to provide support, but enhance it.
- Growth through service: Each interaction, each shared moment of grief or transition, has contributed to my personal and spiritual growth. These experiences have taught me invaluable lessons about compassion, resilience, and the human spirit's capacity for healing. They have reminded me of the privilege of serving others, shaping me into a more empathetic and effective caregiver.
- The ripple effect of kindness: I've seen firsthand how minor acts of kindness and understanding can profoundly affect those we serve. It reinforced my belief in the power of compassionate service to provide immediate comfort and inspire hope and healing that extend far beyond our initial encounter.
- Live every day: It is difficult to ignore that life is temporary when the stream of requests to respond fills your phone. Our time here is

shorter than you expect. Don't let today slip by unnoticed. That is one of the biggest blessings I received by serving.

Reflections on the Holy Spirit

These takeaways have enriched my ministry and life, providing a more profound sense of purpose and fulfillment in my work. They remind me of the privilege of standing beside someone during their most challenging moments, with the transformative power of the Holy Spirit's presence guiding us through.

Observing the Holy Spirit's work in these moments has reinforced my faith in divine guidance. When the words I needed were beyond my training, divine guidance answered my silent prayers for help in ways I never expected.

It has shown me I am not alone, even when I feel inadequate or unsure. The Holy Spirit is always there, guiding, comforting, and providing wisdom beyond my own. It has instilled a sense of peace and confidence in my role.

CHAPTER 2

What If the Incredible Hulk Was There When You Responded and He Was Really, Really Mad?

What you have learned and received and heard and seen in me—practice these things, and the God of peace will be with you.

PHIL 4:9 ESV

SOMETIMES, WHEN I ARRIVE at the scene of a sudden tragedy, anger is the most unmistakable emotion. The anger can be overwhelming, an absolute tidal wave of grief and shock. Many, recognizing me as a chaplain, expect me to offer prayers or cite Scriptures immediately. The appropriate course of action may not always be clear in those first moments. Before anything else, I've always believed I need to earn the trust and respect of those I'm trying to comfort. Letting them speak and allowing them to unleash their pent-up frustrations and questions often becomes my initial role. Why did this happen? How could a loving God allow this? And they frequently asked me similar questions. In those raw moments, I sometimes became the focal point for their anger simply because I was there. Listening without responding immediately, I could sometimes start to make a connection. I would become someone they felt safe opening up to, allowing me the chance to listen and assist genuinely.

Calls to respond come in cryptic messages this time.

My pager read:

- M 7 mo
- CPR
- Address

The sunlight on that Saturday afternoon created a deceptive picture of a perfect day. But the warmth and relaxing atmosphere shattered the moment my pager beeped. The screen flashed an address, along with haunting details: medics were battling to revive a seven-month-old baby boy. Calls like this always bring a unique heartache. The pain of knowing a young life is involved, often affecting everything, including your breathing and heart rate.

As I hit the road, I had the overwhelming hope that the medical team would succeed again. I launched prayers, seeking guidance and strength for them and the right words to say for me as I drove. Realistically, few words can help in times like these. It is more about just being present. I remembered what my son, Devon, often encourages me with: "They may forget everything you say, but they will never forget how you made them feel."

As my mind braced itself for the grim scenario I might encounter, an unexpected beep from the pager shifted my trajectory. Now, dispatch requested my presence in the hospital emergency room. This abrupt redirection kindled a spark of hope in me. Typically, such a change implied that the medics managed to revive the child. They revived the child's heart and breathing. The medics would transport him to the hospital. With every mile I covered driving to the hospital, I clung to that hope, fervently praying for a favorable conclusion to this day.

Approaching the emergency room entrance, I met up with the medics who had initially responded to the call. With the stress in his words, the captain said, "We could not revive Jake, and the medical examiner was in a remote part of the county, so rather than having the family wait two hours for her to arrive, I made the call to transport him." Hearing the captain use the child's name triggered my concern. It suggested he may have developed an emotional attachment to this call.

He delved deeper into the family's intricacies, highlighting the interactions between the parents and their four other kids. But when he came to the father's emotional state, he paused, leaving it unsaid. That silence, that omission, often spoke volumes, leaving me to ponder the unspoken feelings and tensions.

I've noticed that first responders, perhaps as a defense mechanism, sometimes hold back from immersing themselves too deeply in the emotional turbulence. When arriving on a scene, I'd position myself near the command vehicle, waiting for guidance. Every so often, the command would merely gesture toward someone, their subtle shake of the head saying more than words ever could. That reaction was present here.

As I stepped inside, the first thing that struck me was a significant number of police officers. While encounters with law enforcement at the ER weren't uncommon, the sight of four officers standing in pairs signaled that this was no ordinary situation. One officer drew my attention by making a subtle gesture—a slight nod guiding my focus toward a lone figure.

Across the emergency room, I spotted the father. His restless pacing, combined with an unmistakable tension, made his anger clear to everyone. He radiated a fierce determination, but without an outlet he seemed lost, like a caged lion with no way out. It wasn't hard to understand why others hesitated to approach him.

The father's stature was imposing. His size of six feet, four inches combined with his weight-lifting physique was intimidating to all the staff in the emergency room. His massive biceps bulged when he moved his arms, the veins prominent. In addition, he gave the visual impression that he had reached his limit and that the slightest nudge could set him off. As he paced up and down the hallways, clenching and unclenching his fists, he gave the unmistakable impression that he did not want to talk to anyone. He seemed lost in his thoughts.

Extra police were there as a precautionary measure. Even though there were four officers present, I think that dealing with someone with his strength who had utterly lost control would have posed a significant challenge. With no prior information about his background, the staff only used his body language to assess the situation. This ability to gauge someone based on nonverbal cues is something that's swiftly gained when you're involved in handling trauma. Today, it was unmistakable—his prominent neck veins and how he'd tense up whenever anyone came near him. These signs isolated him from everyone else in the emergency room.

From my conversation with them, the medics and police officers were grappling with immense pressure because of the unusually high volume of calls they received that day. The heightened demand for their expertise seemed to cause tension and unease among everyone.

While I was passing by, one officer whispered, "You're on your own, Padre." The officer softly spoke the words, just enough for me to hear. Oddly, this utterance gave me a sense of reassurance, as it seemed to suggest they would watch the situation from a distance.

I may have had a lot of additional doubts if someone had forewarned me about calls like this before I began my work as a chaplain. However, through consistent encounters with the influence and insight that can only stem from the Holy Spirit, I had grown to trust that I would carry that connection with me from now on in ways beyond anything I could imagine.

Navigating tense and unpredictable situations like these can be incredibly challenging, but rewarding. Often, I would hear individuals rely on what they had heard before offering their condolences or perhaps a simple "sorry for your loss" with little thought. It's tough to convey that you genuinely care. I felt most at ease when I introduced myself as Jim and added, "Sorry that you are going through this," then, reaching out to shake his hand. On this occasion, he grasped my hand, and with a firm grip, we shook. Though it was only a firm handshake, I exaggerated my reaction by rubbing and massaging my fingers once he'd let go.

"That may not have been a good idea," I said, looking at him. Initially, he looked confused, but then he seemed to grasp the underlying message with a smile of understanding.

I felt the first thing I needed to do was acknowledge his anger, and I wanted him to know that I had some perception of the emotions and the distress he was experiencing.

"Bill, as I was talking with the officers, I couldn't help but notice your restless pacing in the hallway and the way you clenched your fists. It seems like you want to strike out at something or someone. Am I right?" That was how I started the conversation with him.

He responded with just a nod. As our chat progressed, I hoped my eyes would convey that I noticed the raw hurt in his. "If I could, I'd let you take a swing at me, but I'm not sure I'd hold up."

His response was a brief smile at my comment, slightly easing the tension in his posture for a moment. I stood facing him and the wall, with the activity of the doctors' and nurses' stations behind me, while he leaned against the wall. The unfolding scenes of the ER played out just over my shoulder, giving him a window into today's chaos.

The emergency room at Swedish Hospital is rectangular, with eighteen patient rooms around the perimeter. In the middle were the doctors' and nurses' stations. Today, at each end of the corridor, a pair of officers from the police department stood by, trying to look relaxed. Although they were talking among themselves and with the firefighters who had brought in the child, they were on alert, as I could tell from how they kept glancing in our direction.

As our conversation progressed, I could sense Bill easing up a bit. Pausing, I made a request. "Bill, could you do me a small favor? Just glance over my shoulder and tell me what you notice." Because of where I stood, I couldn't see the activity behind me.

"I see a few doctors and nurses, some firefighters and police officers as well," Bill said.

"Is the nurse outside your son's room visible to you?"

"I see her."

"She had tears in her eyes upon my arrival. I'd rather not be obvious, so I won't turn around to look at her. Can you confirm if she still does?"

"She is blowing her nose and wiping her eyes."

"Bill, before you arrived, she was the nurse who dashed in, cradling your son when the medic unit first pulled up. Every person in this room feels the impact of your loss. The police officers are present because the hospital staff is apprehensive about your reactions as you pace back and forth, clenching your fists."

I felt a flash of an understanding pass through him as he grasped my meaning. Then, I wondered if he might lessen the tension if he said something to an officer. "Maybe if you offered some reassurance, it could diffuse the tension." Looking genuinely apologetic, Bill confessed he was oblivious to how the medical team perceived his presence.

With a nod, he left and approached an officer without saying another word. I watched them talking for a few minutes, but their conversation remained out of earshot. I saw the officer embracing him and offering a comforting pat on the back. During this time, the entire room was quiet. Tension eased, but confusion remained on faces nearby. The doctor nearest me quietly asked what I said to him. I shook my head to let him know I couldn't talk. Bill was coming back to where I stood.

When Bill rejoined me, I asked about his conversation with the officer. He offered, "I told them, I'm sorry, I've never been in a situation like this. The reality is I can't help my son. I can't fix the problem or change the outcome. There is absolutely nothing I can do, and it is tearing me apart."

After asking the nurse for some water, Bill took a sip, then looked at me with a trembling voice and asked what would happen next. As I started to explain the process, he interrupted, talking about his son. I resisted the urge to interject or affirm, choosing instead to simply listen. He paused momentarily, and I waited, letting the silence settle. Then, in that quiet space, Bill slowly revealed Jake's story. By giving him time to gather, Bill could share what had happened earlier that day in his way, at his own pace.

Jake was born prematurely and had to remain in the hospital with extensive complications. He was in critical care and ICU for almost seven months. Jake was their fifth child, and he had two sisters and two brothers, ages six to fourteen. During those seven months, the family would visit the hospital almost daily, and they seldom missed over two days in a row. Initially, they could only watch him through the window. Eventually, they entered the room. During these last months, they could all finally hold him.

Bill reminisced about how Jake would recognize each family member, greeting them with warm smiles whenever they held him. It became a cherished game for them, each trying to elicit the brightest grin from the little one. The long-awaited day finally came. Yesterday was the joyful day Jake came home, marking an end to seven heart-wrenching months of distance. Their hope for normalcy to return was strong.

That afternoon, his wife, Karen, was reclining on the couch, and Jake was resting on her chest. They both fell asleep. She was finally enjoying a moment she had longed for so long, and her nap was peaceful. However, when Karen opened her eyes to look at her son, Jake was blue. She immediately started screaming, and Bill called 911.

That was also when they asked me to go to their home. I was almost at their house when dispatch called to tell me to reroute to the hospital. When I arrived at the hospital, I saw the medics sitting on the tailgate of their rig and the ladder truck crew standing nearby, all speaking softly. I could not hear what they said, but it raised some concerns. It was time for them to restock their rigs, but the expected joking and teasing were missing—our medics, the finest in the nation, work miracles daily. However, losing a battle can get to them, especially for a child.

When rerouted to the hospital, it is usually because the medics got a person's pulse and breathing started again. I have often seen them be successful. Despite the doctor's orders and declaration of death, they persisted. I had expectations that being rerouted today meant they had revived the child.

Shortly after arriving, I discovered the captain had transported the child against the standard protocols. They were supposed to leave the child in place after stopping CPR. No one could touch the child until the medical examiners finished their investigation, including taking pictures and looking for signs of abuse.

Today, the medical examiner was in a distant part of the county, and her estimated arrival time was over two hours. Having your baby on the couch for such a long time without being able to pick him up and hug Jake would be incredibly painful. The parents knew the medical examiner would take the child back to their facility, where they would perform an autopsy. The family would have found it horrible if they could not hold Jake under these circumstances.

Choosing to transport the baby was an act of compassion. Now, in an ER patient's room, Jake remained under the watchful eye of the police, who ensured continued monitoring of the situation. I recognized the importance of maintaining the proper chain of command and contacted the medical examiner. During our chat, I got clearance for the family to hold the child's body until her arrival.

Bill calmed down after hearing my conversation with the medical examiner. I suggested that he be the one to tell his family that he had gotten permission for them to hold Jake. Immediately after that, the kids held Jake while we watched through the door. As we watched, I advised Bill, in the future, to remind each child how Jake would smile during their visits and when it was their time to hold him. It would be helpful if they heard that often. After a short while, I posed a thoughtful question, hoping for a smile. "Who was successful in making Jake giggle the most?" Each sibling claimed ownership for doing that by sharing memories that were precious to them.

I found that simple questions similar to that could change what someone was focusing on, even if initially it was only for a few moments. Later on, those same memories would continue to affect them. Bill could also experience how powerful it would be if he reminded them of the smiles.

The medical examiner, Lauren, arrived, finished interviewing the parents and the other kids, took her photos, and then left, going back out to her truck to get what I expected to be a gurney for the child's remains. However, Lauren didn't return with a gurney and body bag as I assumed. Instead, she had stopped at one of our fire stations and picked up one of the car seats we gave out to new moms. Only after she placed Jake in the car seat and gently set the stuffed animal on his lap did I notice it. I quickly backed out of the room to keep anyone from seeing my reaction.

Believing there is a fine line that allows chaplains to make a difference, I never want to give the impression that I needed help while on a call, but I also hoped the victims and families would sense that I cared and was aware of their pain. Some calls unexpectedly dredged up memories from my history, and it was impossible to predict when those recollections would surface. This time, what I saw in my mind when Lauren placed the stuffed animal on Jake's lap was the picture a Denver Hospital had taken of a stillborn baby boy named Caleb who was also holding a stuffed teddy bear on his lap. Caleb was the first child of my niece.

After a few minutes, I returned to Bill and Karen. It was time to help by providing some options for direction and counseling. They should know certain things that will happen soon. Also, that I'm available to offer resources and support. During this time, I requested that the fire engine crew remain outside with the kids, if possible. The crew was allowing the brothers and sisters to climb all over the engine. Having a personal tour was a helpful distraction for the family and a way for the crew to love on the kids.

They needed to have some plans for when the medical examiner released Jake's remains, how to make the funeral arrangements, and resources for counseling if they wanted to use those. It was never easy talking about funeral stuff at such a difficult time. However, I knew that having some guidance could help relieve some of the stress they would go through.

Once I found Bill and his wife, we went to the hospital's private family room. When we first went in, I kept my head down, reviewing my notes—hoping my eyes would swiftly stop watering.

"How do you handle this?" Bill inquired. Honestly, my heart was hurting for them. I didn't know if I was handling the situation well. Then I looked up at them. They noticed the tears in my eyes. We passed a box of Kleenex around and made some plans during the following hour. Part of our conversation involved the option of grief counseling for the entire family.

My tears had a more significant impact on them than I realized. I received a note card from them a few weeks after that. They pointed out that my tears had helped reassure them they could trust me. In their eyes, I changed from someone just doing their job to someone who sincerely cared about them. God had used the tears I tried to hide. Those tears affected the parents in ways that no amount of words could ever do. They also opened some opportunities to share with the firefighters and police. When I departed, the other children had returned to their parents, and all the first responders were heading back to their station.

While driving home, I got another page to go to Station 11. That station initially responded to the call. When I entered the dayroom, I found both the EMTs and ladder crews present, but it surprised me to see the police from the hospital there as well. Sometimes, after a hard call, I would stop by the stations to be present and available for the responders. First responders rarely want to revisit such events so quickly. Being asked to attend was a surprising request.

The captain gave me a cup of coffee and had me sit in one of their recliners while the others sat or stood around the dayroom in casual conversations. After I sat down, the room became quiet.

"Chaplain, you are not here for us," the captain stated. "This time, we are here for you."

Those words meant a lot to me. It was the best thing I could have heard after being with the family during today's tragedy. Sometimes, after seeing what people are experiencing, it is hard to walk away without being affected.

Insights

- In the role of a chaplain, circumstances don't repeat themselves. Each encounter stands alone, as diverse as the individuals we serve. Each call has various needs, dispositions, reactions, and life backgrounds. The variables at play are too extensive even to attempt cataloging.

- Every call introduces a fresh collection of unique factors, ensuring no hint of routine. Often, I'd silently pray for guidance and insight or the right words to convey at a scene. The help I received would come in various forms—a person's accent, surroundings, interactions with children, or even my personal experiences. What remained constant was the unwavering commitment to serve, reinforced by the belief that the Holy Spirit would accompany me.

- My connection with prayer deepened, lifted by the confirmation of answered prayers. The prayer I relied on most was "Father, help!" However, the meaning went way beyond the two words. I suspect those hearing it might have thought it wasn't complete, or I could not find the right words but needed to say something, and it was my backup.

- Initially, when I considered the title of chaplain, I connected it to someone with a history as a priest or minister. Someone with a seminary education and trained to handle tragic situations. The media sometimes captured them praying with the families or victims of whatever had happened. What was never in that picture was a real estate broker whose primary qualification was loving the Lord and caring about people.

Reflections on the Holy Spirit and the Prayer "Father, Help"

The simplicity and depth of the prayer "Father, help" is like peering into the core of our relationship with Jesus. This prayer is a profound expression of surrender and faith. It's not about presenting a wish list but about seeking connection, guidance, and support in times of need.

In the utterance of "Father, help," there's an implicit acknowledgment of our limitations and an expression of trust in his higher power. It's a recognition that, despite our best efforts, there are moments in life where the path forward is unclear, the burdens too heavy, and the answers seem out of reach. In those moments, turning to God with a heartfelt "Father, help" is both a plea and a declaration of faith.

This prayer embodies the essence of seeking his will. Being an open-ended request, it doesn't impose our desires, but leaves room for the Holy Spirit to guide us. It reflects a willingness to be led and accept outcomes that might be beyond our understanding, but with the trust that they are for our ultimate good. It's about letting go of the illusion of control and embracing the peace that comes from faith.

"Father, help" is a testament to the relationship we seek to have with our God—a relationship not based on transactions or bargains but on trust and the seeking of his will. It's a reminder that we are not alone in our most vulnerable moments. There's a profound strength in the simplicity of this prayer, a strength that comes from acknowledging our vulnerability and trusting in a loving God wiser than us.

The answers to my plea "Father, help" were often immediate and came with surprising clarity, allowing me to connect on a deeper level than expected with the families I served.

CHAPTER 3

Where's Waldo?

Who comforts us in all our affliction, so that we may be able to comfort those who are in any affliction, with the comfort with which we ourselves are comforted by God.

2 Cor 1:4 ESV

ONE BOOK MY KIDS loved when they were little was *Where's Waldo?* My kids were competitive and delighted to be the first to point to Waldo. As I turned to the following pages, scenes changed, and Waldo blended in with the crowd. Then, when you don't expect it, he comes out of the crowd.

The same thing sometimes happens when I arrive on a scene. Someone catches my attention as if the Holy Spirit is looking over my shoulder and pointing at them. Other times, they find me.

My pager read:

- M
- S
- Location was very public

Finding your purpose in some events can be challenging amid the chaos, with sirens blaring and emotions running high. In overwhelming moments, there was always someone I felt directed toward. Be it for comforting words or a silent shoulder to lean on. It's almost like a divine intuition guiding you through the crowd to the person who needed you the most, even if they didn't stand out immediately. The Holy Spirit has a mysterious way of leading us exactly where we need to be. It's incredible how, in the vast sea of faces and noises, someone is reaching out, and somehow, paths cross.

Reading through the dispatcher's brief dispatch, I could immediately sense the challenges offered by the location. Suicide calls come with layers of emotions, deeper and more intricate than in many other situations. For the grieving family and friends, the pain is intense, and blame is often a raw, vocal expression of their anguish. Every memory of their last encounter with their loved one becomes a scene under a microscope as they dissect every word, searching for missed signs.

When I arrived, our Support 7 vehicle was already there.

Support 7 is a small RV donated to the chaplain ministry and converted for our needs. It had a bathroom and two separate sitting areas with tables. It was a safe place to bring in the victims or families.

This vehicle served our ministry well. It shielded people from the weather, and they were not visible to bystanders. It also kept the reporters and camera crews at a distance. Knowing how difficult it was for people to deal with the insensitivity of the press and uninvited crowds at scenes, Support 7 was a safe place.

Also, it worked for law enforcement or, if needed, for interviews without additional distractions. We could also provide refreshments, snacks, coloring books, or stuffed animals for the kids. There are also a lot of other comfort items available, such as water, Gatorade, and protein drinks for rehabbing first responders.

That day, Jim Cudney had parked the RV parallel to the train tracks, only a short distance from the incident site. Jim played a pivotal role as a volunteer, using his skills to convert our RV to fit our unique requirements better. Despite his full-time job, Jim was always on call, ready to respond no matter the hour. Our ministry operated purely on the dedication of volunteers. We had a small team, some serving as chaplains. Our shifts spanned twenty-four hours, running from midnight to midnight. We also had other volunteers who, although not trained as chaplains, contributed to getting the Support 7 RV to the scenes, setting up, and helping meet the physical needs of the victims.

When I got there, the train engineers were already inside our RV. The scene outside was a flurry of activity—police officers, the medical examiner, representatives from several state agencies, and many fire department vehicles. The distant hum of news helicopters heightened the moment's urgency.

As I sat, the engineers began recounting their experience without hesitation. I gently interrupted, letting them know we'd discuss that shortly, but I had an initial question for them. That seemed to catch them off guard, perhaps even unsettling them momentarily, but their demeanor shifted once they heard what I had to ask.

When I sat down, I immediately noticed the absence of their cell phones. "Have you two reached out to your families?" I asked, then added, "Did you leave your phones in the engine?"

One responded, "Yeah, but our supervisor said he'd contact our families on our behalf."

I gently pressed, "How about calling them right now? Hearing your voice might provide some comfort." I placed my cell phone on the table, offering it to them. "Take all the time you need. I'll ensure we give you some privacy."

Their eyes shifted from the phone back to me, and after a brief pause, they nodded in agreement.

Both engineers shared they had experienced "suicide by train" before. It's terrible to experience. It would be hard for them to forget what they saw.

The scene buzzed with so much commotion that holding their focus became challenging. Ultimately, I made the call to move them to the nearby fire station, for a more conducive environment was best. They opened up and shared their feelings more freely in the quieter setting. After an hour, representatives from Burlington Northern arrived at the station to attend to the engineers. With that resolved, I made my way back to the initial scene. The victim's identification and next of kin contact were still unavailable.

While attending to the engineers, an officer handed me a note. It had a woman's name and a contact number scribbled on it. With some urgency, he shared, "She's asked for you specifically. When you can, please reach out to her. She claims to know you and is visibly distressed, with tears streaming down her face." I discreetly hid the note, understanding that I had to focus on resolving the concerns with the engineers.

Returning to the scene, I promptly dialed the number from the note. Wendy identified herself as the voice on the line. Though I strained my memory, I couldn't immediately place her. I've always wished names would stick in my mind better. Through the phone, I could discern the muffled sounds of her tears. The weight of her following words, "I should have known," was unmistakable. They stirred a sense of urgency in me, needing more tangible support than a phone call could offer.

"I think it'd be best if we talked face to face," I gently suggested, inviting her to meet me in my car. "Any officer can direct you to where I'm parked." As she approached, a glimmer of recognition flashed. Despite the passing years, a different scene resurfaced in my memory. Wendy had been there, grappling with the unexpected loss of a close friend. The circle of tragedy, it seemed, had once again ensnared someone she cared for.

"I should've known it," Wendy whispered, her voice steeped in sorrow.

"Known what, Wendy?" I asked gently.

"He would do something like this," she shared, her voice full of emotion.

I took a brief pause, giving her words the weight they deserved. "Why do you feel that way?" I inquired softly.

Lost in her thoughts, she looked away before responding. "I saw him sitting at the table on the top of the embankment when I went for a walk. The look in his eyes seemed so despondent."

Acknowledging her guilt but wanting to offer a different perspective, I softly responded, "Even when we think we know someone inside out, it's challenging to predict such a decision."

Yet, she clung to her guilt, her voice tinged with a quiet despair. "I still believe I should have known."

I leaned in, then asked, "Why do you feel so strongly about that, Wendy?"

She took a deep breath, the weight of years of memories in her eyes. "My daddy committed suicide when I was a teenager." She now appeared to be in her midsixties. The weight with which she marked the years was a poignant reminder of the burden survivors often bear. "After it happened, my mother moved us from Kansas to Washington."

"Was the move primarily to escape from the aftermath of the suicide?" I inquired gently, sensing there might be more layers to her story.

She nodded, "Yes. It was."

"I can't imagine the depth of pain you've experienced because of that," I sympathized. "From what you're sharing, it seems the wound is still raw, even after all these years. And that's okay; everyone processes grief differently. Were you particularly close to your father?"

A soft smile touched her lips, tinged with nostalgia. "Yes, I was a daddy's girl. I thought we were very close."

Curious, I picked up on her choice of words. "Did you always refer to him as 'Daddy'?"

She nodded, "Yes, he was always Daddy. Why do you ask?"

"My daughter has a habit of calling me Daddy," I began, a gentle smile forming as cherished memories played in my mind. "Every time she says it, it feels like a warm embrace. There's something inherently intimate and precious about the title *Daddy*. It carries an innate sense of closeness and vulnerability. It's not a term I encounter often in my interactions after a daughter becomes a teenager. However, when I hear it used, it almost always hints at an unspoken bond that goes beyond the ordinary. And when I heard you use that title for your father, it spoke volumes. It vividly depicted the deep and meaningful relationship you two must've cherished."

"We did," she affirmed, her tone now echoing the depth of their bond.

I paused, weighing my following words with care. "After relocating, especially if it was to distance yourselves from the painful stigma surrounding a family suicide, do you think it might have led to a silence around his memory? Perhaps you didn't discuss him as openly or as often?"

Through countless interactions, I've recognized a recurring pattern in the reactions of loved ones left behind after a suicide. It's strikingly consistent, almost universal. When the survivors recall the person they've lost, the act of suicide often overshadows those memories. Instead of celebrating the individual's life, the weight of their irrevocable act clouds the memories, obscuring the many moments and years before that pivotal point.

"We just—we never really spoke of him afterward," she admitted, her voice in a whisper.

"Do your husband and kids know any details about your father?"

She paused and then shook her head. "They only know he committed suicide. Nothing beyond that."

Intrigued, I asked, "How old was he when it happened?"

She responded, "He was just forty-three."

I paused for a moment, feeling the weight. "May I offer a bit of insight?"

She looked uncertain, her eyes searching mine. "I don't know."

"Wendy, I genuinely believe it might bring some clarity. It will take just a minute. The number of families dealing with suicides might surprise you. It isn't easy to understand what causes someone to take their life or how they justify it at that moment. However horrible the decision was that pushed your dad to take his own life, it was only one decision in his forty-three years. Please do not let that decision keep you from enjoying the great times you shared. You have called him and referred to him as Daddy. It points to a unique, enduring relationship that shaped your early years and who you have become. Have you ever considered separating that one painful decision from the countless cherished memories you have of your dad?" I asked. She paused, her gaze drifting. "It feels impossible. Everything's so deeply connected."

Taking a deep breath, I asked, "Would you be open to trying something with me, just between us, here in the safe confines of this car?"

"What?" she questioned with uncertainty in her eyes.

I took a moment, wanting to approach the subject with the delicacy it deserved. Sensing her hesitation, I began, "It's simple."

Wendy's gaze intensified, waiting.

"Will you tell me about your daddy?" I asked, further encouraging her. "Who was your dad before that day? What are the moments that defined who he truly was to you?"

We settled into a rhythm for the next couple of hours. Wendy's voice wavered between heartache and warmth as she embarked on a sincere journey into her past. Each tale she shared painted a vivid picture of a father who, beyond the shadows of his last act, was steadfast in his love and commitment.

She reminisced about a man who provided for his family and cherished every moment with his daughter. He wasn't just a parent; he was her confidant, her anchor. She brought to life memories of laughter-filled adventures, spontaneous trips, and quiet moments that spoke volumes. Tales of pride, joy, and the bond they shared, and as she talked, her smiles became frequent.

With every word she uttered and every tear she shed, it became clear the anguish of his suicide had buried her childhood memories. After decades, they were resurfacing, gently breaking through the barriers of time and pain.

Wendy's willingness to share her intimate memories with me was a privilege I deeply cherished. Her ability to bring treasured moments from her past into the light affirmed the purpose of my presence that day. I was there in response to a call where the original victim remained unidentified, and attempts to contact the family had been unsuccessful. I realized Wendy was the reason I was there. The significance of her seeking me out did not escape me. Witnessing her reconnection with cherished memories of her father was a profoundly fulfilling experience.

As our conversation wound down, I felt compelled to offer her a gentle nudge toward healing. "Wendy," I started, "would you consider another small favor for me?"

She looked quizzical but open, so I continued, "I've cherished every story you've shared about your daddy. They've truly touched my heart. Might you consider sharing these memories with your husband and children? Let them in on the wonderful moments and the bond you shared with your father. I genuinely believe they'd appreciate and treasure those stories."

When I got home, I stayed in the car to write my report and complete my notes without wanting to be distracted. Going inside my home, Judy, my wife, said, "Did you find the person you were supposed to talk to?"

"No, this time Waldo found me."

It was what she often prayed for when I left on a call. Hearing parts of the stories encouraged Judy as well. Sometimes, the people I expected to reach out to are not obvious amid the chaos and trauma at the scenes.

God often directs my path to be where he wants me to be.

Two weeks after our heartfelt exchange, my phone rang, and Wendy's name appeared on the screen. Eagerly, I answered; her voice was tinted with emotion and her first words reached out to me: "You gave me my daddy back."

Hearing those words had a profound impact on me. The sentiment behind them, the depth of meaning they held, was unmistakable. I know firsthand the unshakable bond a daughter can form with her daddy. It's an enduring connection, one that time or circumstance can sever. Even when life takes one away, the bond remains steadfast.

Having a part in helping Wendy reconnect with her daddy was a wonderful experience.

Insights for Suicides

- Deaths are traumatic: a tragedy for the young but a fitting end for the old. Both bring mourning, but in different ways. When someone succumbs to a prolonged illness, others have a way of offering consoling words:

    ☐ He fought well till the very end.

    ☐ She lived her life to the fullest.

- ☐ What an example he was for completing his journey with grace.

- Statements like these make tragedies sound poetic and ease the healing process for the family members. It puts the deceased in a heroic position and epitomizes their journey for having lived through all seasons. Thus, the loved ones have everything nice and orderly to remember their departed ones in natural deaths. Suicide, in contrast, is a disturbing riddle. Most bystanders and even family members consider it an easy way out, surrendering without a struggle. Yet, who are we to comment without an understanding of their situation and scrutinizing their battle before they ended their life? How long had they been battling the emotional, psychological, or physical torment before making this decision? Or what medications, with their side effects, had instilled suicidal thoughts in them?

- There is a significant contrast in the mourning process following a suicide. Pain is more acute and prolonged than for a natural death. Adjusting to a new normal takes longer than if someone died naturally. Deaths that result from crime, accidents, or wars don't compare with the heartache suicide survivors experience. The families and friends rarely talk about that person after their death, and the ordinary emotions and feelings seldom allow for closure.

- There is also a perceived taboo or stigma associated with suicides. It is not something you want to discuss or openly share with others. Many families hold their feelings and emotions close. Family members are reluctant to share their experiences, even with each other. They become concerned that what they may say will trigger the memories again. When someone takes their life, they leave a slew of unresolved questions and a trail of guilt over the ones close to them.

Reflections on the Holy Spirit

Over time, I realized God introduced every adversity into my life with deeper intent. Even the most painful moments in time circled back, giving me wisdom and perspective. This was especially true of a brutal experience that later became the foundation for my enhanced empathy and connection with families affected by suicide. With this understanding, I approached these families with a gentleness born from personal experience, rather than claiming to understand their pain outright. Instead, I shared I was familiar with the anguish of suicide in a family. It often helped bridge the gap, allowing me to connect and assist in sensitive ways. When families sensed I might genuinely understand a fragment of their heartache, my counsel resonated more deeply with them.

Reflecting on my faith journey, with all its detours, construction zones, and unexpected closures, I can see that these obstacles, once confusing, now make sense as divine reroutings—not just of my path but sometimes of my destination. Seeing God's hand in my past instills a profound trust and confidence in his guidance for my future.

CHAPTER 4

Held Hostage by Insomnia

It's never enough to just tell people about some new insight. Rather, you have to get them to experience it in a way that evokes its power and possibility. Instead of pouring knowledge into people's heads, you need to help them grind a new set of eyeglasses so they can see the world in a new way.

—John Seely Brown

It was 1:30 a.m.; the television offered few choices to pass the time, only reruns of *Friends*, *Barney Miller*, and infomercials selling vacuum cleaners or facial products. My only alternative was a World War II documentary on the USS *Enterprise*. After watching the tales of heroism and the critical importance of the ship in the war, I drifted off to sleep. Then, my pager's abrupt beeping shattered the silence at 4:43 a.m.

My pager read:

- M 84
- Unattended
- Address

It was an overcast morning. The drive to north Edmonds was quiet, save for the barking dogs. As dawn broke, I saw lights twinkling in a few homes, a stark reminder of life's ordinary rhythm contrasting with the situation I was heading into. My prayer en route was to find the words that would comfort a fifty-year-old woman who had just lost her father. Yet, as soon as I arrived and exited my car, two deputies stopped me in the driveway.

"We can't let you go in just yet," the deputy told me.

"What's going on?" I asked. Then, a piercing scream cut through the morning air, making you want to turn away.

"That's the deceased's daughter," a deputy explained. "She's completely lost it, throwing anything within reach."

The deputies shared they had intended to approach her once her initial wave of grief subsided. Her repeated cries of "I didn't mean it" increased my concern for her. Could she pose a danger to herself? Joined by the deputies, we stood just inside the doorway. We could see her grief as she hurled objects against a wall. I stood there, frozen, grappling with how to reach her.

In the early days of my chaplaincy, the sense of being out of my depth led to frequent internal concerns. However, it also enriched my prayer life. I made a straightforward and heartfelt plea: "Father, help! Amen." Over time, the consistent answers to this prayer built my confidence, reassuring me I was never alone. After a while, I grew eager to witness the Holy Spirit's work, often exhibited through unexpected recollections of past events. Sometimes, a home's décor would trigger a long-forgotten memory, or the lyrics of a song would all suddenly make sense during my visit. Other times, I could sense something was off, but I couldn't quite put my finger on it. In these moments, further silent prayers would often bring clarity and direction.

Confronted with the daughter's violent outburst, "I didn't mean it!" I perceived her actions as being more self-directed than aggressive. She continued her rampage, shattering a glass against the wall, then hurling a book, pursued by another cup, and whatever else she could grasp. The living room was descending into a mess. It was my first encounter with such an extreme display of grief, but it wouldn't be the last. Her intense reaction, rooted in the agony of losing her father, was beyond judgment. In such instances, there are no guidelines or definitive coping strategies.

Her continuous cries of "I didn't mean it!" hinted at a profound connection with her father, yet also hinted at a deep regret or unresolved issue. Amid her turmoil, an idea presented itself as she reached for another coffee cup. With a calm yet assertive tone, I inquired, "Could you please make us some coffee?" The request was out of place amidst the turmoil, but it was one I had found effective before.

She paused, her gaze fixed on me, the cup still in her hand. Then, almost mechanically, she lowered her hand and walked toward the kitchen without uttering a word. Watching in disbelief, the deputies, who had hesitated to engage with her and were waiting for her to calm down, looked on. The sudden cessation of her screams and the abrupt end to the chaos surprised them.

The deputies remained vigilant and ready to intervene if necessary. They expected a prolonged ordeal, yet she surprised them by calming down. Witnessing her transition from intense emotion to quiet, methodical actions was remarkable.

The officers' expressions mirrored their readiness for her to persist, perhaps with more outbursts or chaos. Instead, she walked away to make coffee like any other ordinary day. It was astonishing how a mundane inquiry about coffee could bring someone back from emotional turmoil to a place of quiet.

Following her into the kitchen, I gently asked, "Could you share what you didn't mean?" Her movements were deliberate and unhurried as she began brewing coffee in silence. Eventually, she turned toward me, holding two steaming cups, and motioned for me to join her at the table.

"My father asked to see his mother this morning," she began, her voice quivering. "He was eighty-four and hadn't been out of bed for a while. He longed to see her again, but she passed away fifteen years ago. I said yes this time when he asked, instead of correcting him. Then, just five minutes later, he stopped breathing. I know I told him he could go, but I didn't mean for him to die. I want him back," she broke down, tears cutting through her grief.

Allowing her words and sobs to fill the space between us, I waited for a moment. My response to her was, "Deep down, I don't think you do." Her eyes, brimming with tears, met mine. Then, whispering, "I know, but I miss my daddy so much already."

Giving a subtle nod to the deputies, I signaled everything was under control and they could leave if they wished. They exited soon after, leaving Deborah and me alone to await the funeral home's attendants.

Over the next hour, as we waited, Deborah shared some of her favorite memories of her dad. During those moments of reflection, I asked her how her parents met. She told me a story of a young sailor meeting his future wife in Hawaii during shore leave in World War II. Sharing his story was a tale that seemed to bring her comfort, a reminder of happier times amidst the sorrow.

Letting her know I was listening, I asked, "Deborah, what ship had he served on?" Her answer, the aircraft carrier *Enterprise*, startled me. My insomnia had made it a long night, but hearing her answer made me understand why God had not let me sleep.

Then, inquiring, "Did he ever open up to you about his experiences and memories from the war?" "Daddy would never talk about it!" She emphasized her answer.

I had learned from other calls that this was a typical response from the families of veterans who had been in combat. They did not want to talk about what they had been through or seen. It could cause them to relive the events they tried hard to forget.

But the family members wanted to know, hoping it would provide a better understanding of the veteran. Hearing stories about what the veteran went through, no matter the source, would be a treasure to the children of those who served in the battles. Being with the families of someone who served in combat was always an honor. However, this was even more so because of what I had learned in the documentary just a few hours before.

One of my jobs involved estimating the weight of the deceased person and assisting the funeral home in determining the number of people required. As I stood over and looked at the earth suit for "Daddy," I thought about what I had seen on TV. Lying before me was a man who had experienced it all in the years he served on the *Enterprise*. I could see no photos, medals, or anything else on the walls even hinting at his time aboard that ship. Yet, he was part of history. The *Enterprise* was a critical piece in the Battle of Midway, and because of the part his ship had played, it altered world history. This morning, I stood beside someone who had served during the pivotal battle and changed the war's course with Japan. It was humbling.

I had seen a Bible in the home when I first arrived. That led me to ask if I could pray over her daddy. She just nodded. I don't think she was expecting my words as she heard me thanking him for his service and was thankful that the experiences that had remained in his mind from that time would now be gone forever.

When I finished, I wondered aloud, "Would you like to know more about the aircraft carrier *Enterprise*? Some stories about the *Enterprise* could offer insight into what happened earlier today by providing additional insight into your daddy. I believe I am supposed to share them with you. You will understand why in a moment." She had a puzzled look on her face now. That was the first time I had ever suggested anything like this.

I described my night, explaining that I had finally fallen asleep after watching the TV documentary, when the page came in this morning. The subject of the documentary was the aircraft carrier USS *Enterprise* and its pivotal role during World War II. It started at 1:30 a.m. and ran until 3:00 a.m. I got paged for this call two hours later.

Those stories from the *Enterprise* were not just about a ship or the battles it was in. They were also about the men who served and their shared experiences. The camaraderie forged in the fires of war. These sailors are not only bound by their duty, I continued, but by a bond of brotherhood stronger than steel and more profound than the ocean. "Your father was among those brave souls." As she listened, I could see the pride on her face.

I shared some of the first-person accounts of sailors who were aboard. Especially the ones that would shed light on some heroes who had served on that ship. One part of the documentary said many times that mortally wounded sailors had continued to struggle to pull shipmates out of harm's way after bombings, torpedoes, or kamikaze assaults. The sailors would not succumb to their wounds until they knew their shipmates were out of harm's way.

At that moment, she understood how that related to her father. How telling her dad that he could go may have given him the peace that she would be okay after he died. She had blamed herself for her father's death, even though she wasn't responsible. So, I wanted her to realize she may have done her dad a favor; by permitting her dad to see his mother, she may have freed him from the hospital bed that held him captive. It could have allowed him peace and stopped him from struggling, which was an incredible gift.

After calling a funeral home and waiting for the attendants to come and transport his earth suit, I remained on the scene for a while longer. Deborah continued to share more stories about her daddy. How she talked about her father and conveyed her grief touched my heart. Seeing her improve from when I first arrived was rewarding, and I silently thanked God for giving me the courage to follow his lead. Finally, she bid me goodbye with a big hug.

I started my car and backed out when another thought crossed my mind. I love the way the Holy Spirit gets my attention. Turning off the engine, I walked back and knocked on the door. Standing in the doorway, I asked her if she had seen the movie *Titanic*. She had.

"Do you remember the ending?"

"Kind of," she replied, "the woman died."

"Yes! But do you remember what happened after that?"

"I thought that was the end," she told me.

"I would like to describe what happened after that part. May I? Do you remember her being buried at sea?"

"Not really."

"Then allow me to describe it. After that, the director had a scene depicting her entering one of the *Titanic* companionways. It showed lots of destruction, decay, and debris; the color was a drab, greenish monotone. But the further she went along the corridor, things changed. The teak decks began changing color as she proceeded down the companionway, becoming restored to their original condition. The paintings reappeared on the walls, and deck chairs emerged, looking new and inviting."

She nodded.

"Then, as the camera comes around the corner, someone in a tuxedo is holding the door open, and an endless reception line comes into view, with all the people dressed in their finest clothes. It included all those who had gone down with the ship or died since it sank. They were all applauding, smiling, and nodding as she entered. Then she continued up the stairs where her boyfriend, Jack, awaited. His hand goes out to her, and she takes it. Then the camera swings around, and for the first time, it shows Kate. She is in her prime and appears in perfect health."

"Exactly! Yes," she recalled.

"I wonder if you could, instead of seeing Jack when you close your eyes, picture Jesus with his arm reaching out, and instead of Kate, your dad reaching back?" That started her tears again.

"My thought is if a movie director down here can come up with such an incredible reunion for those who had gone on before, then just imagine how much more breathtaking the reunion of your parents is when God, their Creator, has planned it out."

I watched her lips curl up into a smile over the thought, and I could see the description's impact on her. A few hours ago, she blamed herself for her part in her dad's death, but that changed as she pictured her parents together in heaven.

It was another God moment for me. How unexpected that I could recall the ending scene of the *Titanic* in such vivid detail after so many years and seeing it only once.

God was building in me the confidence I would have or already had everything I needed. I just needed to step out in faith and meet him there. When I followed up with her later, she told me she had watched the *Titanic* again, and the last scene of the movie meant more to her than I could have imagined. Her face lit up with pure delight as she embraced her father's passing.

Helping someone transition past the initial pain of loss is very rewarding. It provides satisfaction that God has used me and confirmation that I am serving where I should.

Insights

- Everyone is unique in how they handle personal tragedies. There is no "normal" to their behavior or reactions. No rules apply. It is just the way they are grieving now. They are trying to cope with a complex emotional situation, yelling, screaming, throwing things, or being silent and stoic; anything can happen. Victims and survivors often feel the need to be doing something, and frequently responders too.

- They might feel compelled to make calls to arrange a funeral, look for wills and insurance policies, and some may just be pacing from room to room. The simple task of brewing coffee has proven to slow them down enough to allow for more meaningful conversations. It gives them something physical to do and does not require much thought. I use the time while the coffee is brewing to let them know that, in most situations, nothing needs to happen immediately other than a few phone calls to family and close friends.

- I let them know I will send them a checklist of some tasks that will come up in the following weeks. Knowing they will receive that list and have a place to start is helpful. Without them being still for a few minutes, it would be challenging to have these conversations. Making coffee has been an excellent tool for me, even if I seldom actually drink the coffee.

- As I backed out of the driveway, I wondered if he would see his shipmates again. It was the first time I used the description of the end of the movie *Titanic*. Besides his mom, relatives, and friends, I thought he would also see the sailors who had served with him. We don't know what exactly happens after someone dies, so I felt comfortable suggesting this. It was an easy correlation for me to adapt and use. I have used the *Titanic* story many times over the years in situations. The fact is that we struggle to imagine or visualize heaven. Or what will it be like when we reunite with others who have already passed away? References to the pearly gates, streets of gold, glorious mansions, or similar are hard for most to visualize.

Reflections on the Holy Spirit

I can't take credit for recalling the end of the *Titanic*, having only seen the movie once. I believe it was a thought placed in my mind by the Holy Spirit. The director's description of what a glorious reunion might look like has helped many families. For the surviving family and friends, it helped. They now have a mental image of a glorious reunion where their loved one would be the guest of honor. Of course, the emotions of grief and loss are still present, but there is also joy at what the loved one may experience in a new body without pain.

Serving as a chaplain requires embracing being with total strangers amid unpredictable physical and emotional upheavals. Preparation for the unknown is impossible; instead, it's about trusting that the Lord will equip you. A readiness to adjust to God's will often defines our role. Confidence in this identity doesn't come quickly, but it strengthens more through real-life practice than theoretical training. The measure of a pastoral or caregiver's abilities and limits only becomes apparent when faced with the challenges and crises God uses for their growth. Like silver, the effectiveness of a chaplain increases with refining.

CHAPTER 5

The Heaviest Burden I Carried: Twelve Pounds, Three Ounces

> I used to ask God to help me.
> Then I asked if I might help Him.
> I ended up by asking God to do His work through me.
> —Hudson Taylor

> Bear one another's burdens, and so fulfill the law of Christ.
> —Gal 6:2 ESV

It was a message felt by both sides of the siren. Amid these intense encounters, some calls resonate more profoundly than others, echoing the duality of our role in both comforting the afflicted and supporting those who serve. One such call came just as the day was yielding to night.

The sun had just begun setting when my pager displayed its cryptic text.

My pager read:

- M 3 mo
- CPR

- Address

Those few characters painted a vivid and distressing picture in the realm of chaplaincy: a three-month-old boy, a desperate attempt to revive him. Messages like this touch your heart.

As I sped toward the address, a familiar flurry of questions swirled in my mind. These queries were not just about the specifics of the unfolding tragedy, but about the unseen ripples it created:

- How many lives were changing at this very moment?
- Would I find parents in the grip of unimaginable grief or first responders wrestling with the fragility of the life they work hard to save?
- Is this their cherished firstborn?
- Had they faced the struggles of conception before this?
- Were there siblings waiting at home, too young to comprehend the chaos?
- Might it have been a tragic accident?
- What would the state of their home reveal about the preceding moments?
- Would I encounter a gathering of family and friends, all searching for answers?
- Would I witness the harrowing blame shared between devastated parents?
- Also significant is how this would affect the first responders, those on the front lines.

Each call, especially those involving children, brings its own tapestry of emotions, challenges, and profound questions. As I navigated the roads, I prepared myself for the scene I would encounter and the emotional and spiritual support I would need to provide in those critical first moments and also beyond.

The delicate dance of law enforcement protocol, while necessary, can sometimes amplify the anguish in already devastating circumstances. Especially in cases involving child fatalities, the guidelines are stringent. No one may touch or move the child until the medical examiner arrives. Their job entails interviewing every family member present, documenting everything, capturing photographs, and undertaking a thorough site investigation. Procedures aim for objective clarity, yet amid raw grief, they feel impersonal.

Arriving at the scene, a sheriff greeted me, his face etched with concern. He explained the heart-wrenching situation unfolding inside. Once the medics had ceased CPR, the distraught mother, driven by an overwhelming wave of grief, clutched her child and refused to let go. Out of respect for her grief, the officers hadn't forced separation but had requested she remain stationary on the couch. The sheriff's eyes searched mine, a silent plea for help. "Can you do anything to help her comply?"

As I stepped into the living room, the first fifteen seconds were telling. The atmosphere was heavy, laden with tension, yet every detail stood out in stark clarity—the kind that only moments of intense emotion can bring. The father sat isolated to my left, fifteen feet from his wife. He appeared to be lost in another world, his gaze fixed on his phone screen, using it as a refuge from the crushing reality around him.

Ahead, the centerpiece of the scene was the mother. She sat on an expansive sectional sofa, cradling her baby to her chest. Their bond was visible as she rocked back and forth in a soothing rhythm for their comfort. In between her rocking, she'd shoot a fierce, piercing glare at the police officer standing nearby, who, with a tone of gentle insistence, kept asking her to lay the baby down. Her glances would also land on her husband. Each one carried a mix of despair, anger, and pleading when they did.

The home was affluence, every item in its place. It contrasted with the chaos of emotions that had taken over its inhabitants. Absent were any signs of other children. Further adding to the scene's complexity, a medic remained sitting on the couch. His repeated apologies echoed in the quiet room. Two other firefighters stood by. Their continued presence was unexpected and hinted at the significant impact of the situation once the time of death was called. Overseeing it all was the battalion chief.

Unsure who to talk to first, I moved a kitchen chair near the mother, hoping it might prompt the father to close the distance and sit beside his wife. She abruptly turned away when I asked if I could see her child.

I assured her I had no intention of separating her from her child. Then, after studying my gaze, she revealed the baby's face. The sorrow in the room was tangible.

"He's beautiful. What is his name?" I was always careful not to refer to a victim in the past tense.

"Brady," she whispered back.

A memory surfaced for me, and I shared, "Brady was our second choice when considering our son's name."

She seemed to relax just a little after my answer. A faint curiosity lit her eyes. "What name did you finally choose?"

"Devon."

She managed a slight nod. "I like that name."

Hoping to offer some semblance of support. "The reason I'm here is to be a liaison for you. If there's anything you need, please let me know. May I ask your name?"

"Debby," she said.

Despite my invitation for him to join us, the father stayed in his chair, a silent figure enveloped in his own world, unresponsive to what was happening around him. His stoicism was unmistakable. Excusing myself from Debby, I moved my chair closer to him. His name, I learned, was Kevin. Reading his body language as he refused to make eye contact, it became clear pushing for a conversation at this moment would be ill-advised.

In this delicate moment, discretion was paramount. I sought Battalion Chief Steve for a deeper understanding of what happened, and he led me to the kitchen, signaling the need for privacy with a gesture. In the quiet space, Steve revealed Kevin had become overwhelmed with desperation, begging the firefighters to increase their efforts for his son. This outburst happened while Debby remained outside, unaware of the intense emotions unfolding within. Kevin reached a heartbreaking climax when he overheard the doctor instruct the medics to halt their resuscitation attempts. He became engulfed with grief and uncontrollable tears. The Chief also shared that Kevin had been the one who discovered his son lifeless in the crib. Frantic, Kevin dialed 911 and, with the dispatcher's guidance, tried to breathe life back into Brady.

I told the Chief I also had concerns for the firefighter, Jason, who had remained on the couch. Steve shared Jason had a child who was just two days older than Brady. This call had hit him hard; he wanted to stay there for the family until I arrived.

Leaving the BC, I asked Jason if he could help me. I did not wait for an answer but went outside to the deck off the kitchen, where no one could hear us. Once out, I asked him if there was anything that he felt might be helpful if I knew. He confirmed the father was performing CPR when they arrived and was very involved until he heard the doctor on the radio tell them to stop. After, he did not go to his wife, just to his chair. I expressed

The Heaviest Burden I Carried: Twelve Pounds, Three Ounces

my gratitude for his insight and help, but we stayed in the kitchen, chatting with the sheriff about his shift. Part of me was looking for a brief break from the emotional weight in the next room.

When Lauren arrived, she introduced herself as the medical examiner and asked if the mother would set the baby down on the couch while she asked some questions. The mother held Brady even tighter, and her body language said that would not happen. Then, Lauren asked if the mother could help with the exam without letting go of him, and she agreed. The mother uncovered, but still cradled, Brady. After about forty-five minutes, Lauren finished with the photos and had the information she needed. Now it was time to take Brady back to her facilities.

However, Debby would not let go, and it became very awkward. I learned later she had heard the sheriff mention they would do an autopsy. But to her, that meant they would dissect her baby.

Lauren stands out as the most compassionate and considerate medical examiner I've been with on the scenes. Noticing my connection with Debby, Lauren asked me to join her in another room. She intended to propose to Debby that I was the one to hold Brady. Before doing so, she wanted to ensure I would be comfortable. However, it was my suggestion that I be the one to ask Debby. I couldn't have foreseen how much that choice would resonate with me afterward.

Rejoining Debby, I sat beside her as Lauren stepped outside, giving us space. In the room's quiet, I delicately proposed the idea of her letting me hold Brady. I can never forget the depth of her gaze as she looked at me while considering my request. Then, without a word, she extended her arms, offering Brady to me. Her eyes reflected an agonizing mix of pain and the unexpected trust in a stranger. I was cautious not to rush this moment, hoping that the gentleness of my holding Brady would reassure her. We continued our conversation while sitting on the couch with Brady nestled in my arms, until it felt the time seemed right.

"Debby, would you allow me to carry Brady out now?"

"I guess so."

Standing up, I asked Kevin if he wanted to hold Brady again, but he only shook his head without looking up.

"Debby, would you mind walking me to the door?"

"I would like that."

Once at the door, she kissed Brady one last time. I found Lauren, out of sight, waiting around the corner of the house, and handed Brady to her.

Upon reentering the room, the sight of them navigating their intense grief, although only separated by fifteen feet, felt like they were worlds apart. Being aware of the grim statistics concerning marriages faltering after a child's loss weighed on me. I resolved to do everything I could to not leave them like this.

Once all the responders had left, tension continued to fill the room. Debby shot Kevin piercing glances while he fixed his eyes on his phone or the floor, avoiding her gaze. I edged my chair nearer to Kevin, hoping to bridge the emotional distance that had grown between them.

"Kevin, you look like you have something on your mind, but the words are just out of reach," I opened.

"There's nothing to say. I messed up. Brady might still be alive if I'd followed the 911 dispatcher's instructions better. I tried to do the CPR like she told me, but what I did was not comparable to how the medics did the CPR when they got here."

His words took me by surprise. "Do you recall how long it took them to arrive?"

"Just three or four minutes, I think. Their station is just around the corner."

"And Debby? Was she assisting with the CPR?"

"No, as soon as I had 911 on the phone, she stepped outside to wait for the medics."

His words provided a crucial piece of the puzzle concerning their emotional disconnect. Debby had been outside during Kevin's desperate attempts at CPR and didn't see firsthand his struggle to save their child. By the time she returned, Kevin had retreated to the recliner, wrestling with self-imposed guilt over whether he had done it right or hard enough. This might explain the physical and emotional distance he maintained from her. On top of that, Kevin confided he couldn't bring himself to hold Brady, afraid it would make the unbearable reality all too real.

Knowing from experiences, Kevin needed to view his actions more compassionately. He needed to understand that the medics who arrived were among the best in the country, and they reached the scene in under four minutes. If anyone had the skills and expertise to revive Brady, it was this team. Kevin couldn't have outperformed them or done anything more effectively by himself than what he did.

Debby heard Kevin from across the room as he shared with me and moved closer, sitting cross-legged on the floor next to him. She grabbed his hand and held on, even though he tried to pull away. I attempted to communicate the medic's skill came from lots of repetitive training. I hoped to move on to another subject rather than let him get stuck rethinking everything, so I asked, "Is there something I should tell the dispatcher you talked with that might help her in the future?" Then I waited while he processed his answer.

Kevin looked thoughtful for a moment, then expressed his gratitude for her composed demeanor during the chaotic event. "She remained calm within all the chaos and my screaming," he acknowledged. Pausing, he continued, "I can't think of much else she could've done with me." He made a simple request, "If you get a chance, please thank her for me."

The following conversation was because of the training and insight I had received, both at the Chaplain Academy and also during our weekly team meetings to debrief at breakfast on Wednesday mornings, when the topics we discussed were about the difficulties couples faced after a child's death.

I opened with, "Kevin and Debby, I know this is an unimaginably difficult time for both of you. Everyone processes grief differently, but there's something vital I want to share with you."

Kevin: "What's that?"

"When we face such profound pain, there is a natural instinct to retreat, to protect our emotions, maybe even hold things back because we don't want to burden others or confront our feelings."

Debby only nodded.

"But pulling away, especially from each other, can create a distance that's hard to bridge later. It's essential to lean on one another during this time."

Kevin: "I just don't want to upset Debby further."

Debby: "And I don't want to make things harder for Kevin."

"You see what just became apparent? It is the power of communication and connection. You both have been on opposite ends of this room, trapped in your reflections and perhaps misinterpreting each other's needs and actions. But through open dialogue, you both formed a bridge, getting a few steps closer to one another. Remember this moment and seek that bridge whenever you feel that distance growing again. Use words, touch, or even a shared silence, but always attempt to reconnect. Grief can isolate, but love and understanding can bridge any distance."

"I understand your fears, and your intentions are loving. But remember, you both are going to struggle to go through this. Sharing, even the painful parts, can bring help. It's okay to grieve separately, but also find moments to grieve together."

Debby: "It's just so hard to find the words."

"Sometimes, words aren't necessary. A hug, a comforting touch, or just sitting together in silence can convey so much. And when you're ready to speak, be honest. It's okay to be vulnerable with each other."

Kevin: "I want to be there for Debby, but I'm struggling."

"And that's okay, Kevin. It's not about having answers or being strong all the time. It's about being present and open. Sharing your struggles allows Debby to support you, and vice versa. Remember, love is as much about leaning on each other as it is about holding each other up."

Kevin: "Thank you for reminding us."

They were sitting together, hugging and sobbing as I left.

Hours Later, at SnoCom Dispatch Center

I arrived at SnoCom, the local dispatch center, and discovered Sara was on the other end of Kevin's frantic call, guiding him through the CPR process. For dispatchers like Sara, their role concludes when first responders arrive. They are no longer informed about the results of the situations they were engaged in. This absence of closure can weigh on them. Recognizing this, I wanted to convey to Sara that her guidance had given the baby the best possible chance at survival, hoping that this knowledge might offer her some consolation and closure. Closure is such an odd word for something like this.

The supervisor had already removed Sara from the board, and I met her in the break room. I passed along Kevin's comments about how she handled his call and how staying on the line until the medic arrived helped. The difference in her was visual as she sat up in her chair. Leaving SnoCom, I saw her heading back to the board to finish her shift.

Insight

- Fifteen Seconds. Picture yourself arriving at a scene where the officer updates you on the situation, providing details about what has occurred, who is present, and who will arrive. They then lead you into the home. The sergeant introduces you as their chaplain, and all eyes turn to you. The family is not sure why you are there, so they expect you to justify your presence. At this moment, you may feel like an intruder, their skepticism palpable.

- You now have fifteen seconds, to assess the room, and you must read the subtle cues in people's body language and facial expressions, observe their interactions, and note the home's décor—all without breaking eye contact. The family is waiting for you to say something that shows you care. The first words you speak can set the tone if you will have an impact.

- In those crucial first fifteen seconds, seize the opportunity to show genuine concern. Strive to earn their trust, reassuring them that your sole purpose is to offer support. My own experiences with personal tragedies often provided a foundation for empathy, allowing me to connect with others facing similar challenges.

- Word choice can be pivotal in emotionally charged situations. The terminology can influence a family's perception and response. For instance, I opt for *exam* over *autopsy*. While families often recognize the nuances between the terms, the use of *exam* lands softer, conveying a hope that a complete autopsy would not be necessary.

Reflections on the Holy Spirit

Personal experiences are both a gift and a burden, especially in moments like these. They can offer unique insights, even as they weigh on the heart. By the time I was twenty-four, Judy and I had faced the heartbreak of five miscarriages. The insights gained from those painful experiences later helped me assist others in ways I could never have imagined. I didn't need to recall those memories. They were just there, and allowing me to see how the Holy Spirit used those events to benefit others was a blessing.

This is the prayer I often offered as I left my car and stepped into the surrounding chaos: "Father, don't let me get in your way." There is trust in this prayer. Acknowledging that I don't have the answer opens the door for the Holy Spirit to intervene and be my guide.

CHAPTER 6

It Depends

Firefighters are some of the only people who run toward danger instead of away from it and still manage to keep a sense of humor. We find a way to laugh even when the heat is on. It's our way of keeping the flames at bay.

—Unknown

Maria was one of those rare souls you rarely encounter these days. She possessed a selfless heart, always ready to extend a helping hand, irrespective of her own struggles or sorrows. The day we met, her world had crumbled, yet her spirit of generosity remained unshaken.

My pager read:

- M 63
- UA
- Address

When I arrived at the scene, the medics were wrapping up their duties. They moved with a practiced efficiency, collecting their tools and equipment, and were a few minutes from departing from Maria's rented condo. The hospital bed where Maria's husband lay still dominated the room, his journey having reached its end.

Maria was on the floor, a few feet from the foot of the bed, her grief finding a voice in moans and wails that echoed through the sparse room and beyond. The battalion chief introduced me, which had no effect on her sobbing and wailing, which I had expected. I cleared a space and sat on the floor near her, to be at eye level, hoping to offer some solace.

Trying to calm her seemed futile at first. But amidst her sorrowful cries, a moment of connection occurred. She caught the concern in my eyes, and something shifted. Her expression transformed as she offered me a smile, a fleeting respite from her grief. She then explained to me, with surprising clarity and lack of emotion, that in her Filipino culture, this vocal expression of grief was a way of honoring the departed. This revelation caught the medics and me off guard.

After sharing this piece of her world with us, she returned to her moans, embracing her cultural rites with renewed intensity. Time seemed to stretch on, each moment weighted with her sorrowful moans. Then, as if a silent alarm had rung, signaling that she had fulfilled her duty of mourning, she ceased.

In the stillness that followed, Maria asked if we could pray together. What began as a prayer of mourning transformed into prayers of gratitude and praise, a testament to her resilient faith.

When I inquired if there was anything I could do for her, her immediate concern was not for herself, but for the boxes of vitamins and supplements she had accumulated to aid her husband. She hoped that the vitamins and supplements would be beneficial to someone who needed them.

I didn't realize then that I was about to embark on a journey to help and witness the profound depths of human generosity in the face of immense personal loss. Maria's act of giving in her grief was a powerful testament to her character—a soul so profoundly rooted in caring for others that even in her darkest hour, she thought of how she could help someone else.

Maria, her eyes reflecting a mix of hope and urgency, implored me to reach out to food banks, shelters, churches—anyone who might benefit from the vitamins and supplements. She was determined that we shouldn't discard them and believed that they held the potential to aid others, just as she had hoped they would help her husband.

As our conversation meandered, Maria kept circling back to the topic of the vitamins with a persistence that spoke volumes about her character. With a hopeful sparkle in her eyes, she insisted I should be the one to distribute them. I know firsthand how hard it is to get anyone to accept pills of any kind, even if they are in the original unopened boxes.

Maria's insistent, hopeful gaze overshadowed my initial reluctance about dealing with the supplements. She seemed to see in these boxes not just pills and potions, but a legacy of care that could still serve a purpose. So, I finally agreed.

Looking up from our conversation, I noticed the medics who were across the room and standing behind the kitchen island. They wore smiles, hinting at an unshared knowledge. Earlier, I learned Maria had offered these items to the medics. She also wanted them to take the hospital bed, sheets, and pillows along with the unused prescriptions and the exercise weights her husband once used. The desire to find purpose in every remnant of her husband's battle with cancer was strong.

One of the medics inquired about the location of my car and took my keys. I then discovered the reason for their smiles: he bent down behind the kitchen island and stood up with a two-foot square box. Setting it on the counter, he stacked another on top while the other medic did the same before heading to my car. They each made another trip, and when they came back, we all thought that was the end of the supplements.

Hearing them say they had finished moving the cartons to my car, Maria's reaction was swift and decisive. She sprang into action, her movements infused with a mixture of determination and relief. She swiftly pulled the medics into the bedroom, her energy almost contagious. When they reappeared, the change in the atmosphere was palpable. Maria's face was a canvas of delight, her eyes shining with gratitude and triumph. The medics, holding additional cartons of supplements, were trying hard to maintain a professional demeanor, but the corners of their mouths betrayed a smirk.

I remained with Maria, trying to offer words of comfort and support, but my mind was partially outside, imagining the growing pile of cartons in my Tahoe.

The scene soon turned almost comical. One by one, the medics returned, each time carrying out more cartons, their faces lit up with uncontainable delight. They seemed to be in on a joke I was just beginning to understand. They briskly moved past me, each firefighter carrying multiple cartons in their arms, as I attempted to voice my concerns about the sheer volume of supplements, but they paid no attention to my words in their good-natured hustle.

The sight outside was something to behold: my Tahoe, once spacious and empty, now crammed with boxes stacked to the ceiling. The firefighters' efficiency in packing was commendable, albeit overwhelming. They had transformed my vehicle into a veritable fortress of health supplements.

Maria, meanwhile, continued to talk, her voice a steady stream of gratitude and instructions, unaware of my growing apprehension. The firefighters, in contrast, were fully aware and thoroughly enjoying every moment. Their smiles grew wider with each trip to my car, each box adding to their amusement.

Then, just when I thought we had reached the peak of this surreal situation, Maria emerged with the box of Depends. Her presentation of this almost full box, as if it were a treasured item, was both touching and overwhelming. The firefighters quickly seized the opportunity for more jest and assured me that my car still had space—on the passenger seat. The firefighters moved my personal items to the floor unceremoniously to make room.

With a mixture of resignation and bemusement, I watched as someone placed the box prominently on the passenger seat, positioning its label outward like a billboard advertisement. The firefighters' laughter echoed around us, a lighthearted endnote to a task that had started as a simple act of kindness.

The task of finding new homes for the vitamins and supplements turned into a journey in itself. I must have contacted dozens of organizations—charities, churches with food banks, outreach ministries—but to my dismay, none would take them. I couldn't help but notice the irony of the situation.

These cartons became my unlikely companions, occupying space in my car because they wouldn't fit in my garage. The gigantic box of Depends continued to ride shotgun during my travels. The sheer volume and variety of the supplements made finding them a new home increasingly challenging. It wasn't until I broadened my search to churches in neighboring cities that I finally found a willing recipient who took pity on me and took the supplements.

The Depends, however, were a different story. Their presence in my life took on a comical, almost surreal quality. Since the box was open, I discovered I couldn't donate them, which left me pondering their fate. Eventually, I found a spot in my garage, tucked away but not forgotten. I harbored a playful plan to repurpose them as a white elephant gift for the firefighters at Christmas, a humorous nod to their ongoing jests.

This plan, however, took an unexpected turn when my grandkids discovered them. Their delight in teasing me about the giant box of Depends added another chapter to the saga. Their laughter and jokes filled the garage, a lighthearted reminder of the unexpected paths our actions can take.

Then, one day, a mishap occurred as I was working on an antique car. Oil spilled across the garage floor. In my search for kitty litter to soak up the spill, my wife, Judy, innocently inquired about the commotion. Upon explaining the predicament, she, with the practical wisdom often found in nurses, suggested using the Depends. Her suggestion, though unorthodox, turned out to be remarkably effective. The Depends, originally a source of amusement and mild frustration, found a new purpose in the most unexpected way.

This entire experience, from the initial overwhelming donation to the unexpected use of the Depends, became a series of anecdotes shared among family, friends, and the fire crew. Each retelling added layers to the story, transforming it from a simple act of charity into a tale rich with humor, human connection, and the unpredictable nature of life's journey.

The saga of the Depends took another unexpected turn, adding yet another layer to the story. After using them for the oil spill, they ended up on our garage floor for a few days. Eventually, Judy, ever practical, decided it was time to dispose of them. She placed the oil-soaked Depends in our community's large waste disposal bin.

The next time I went to take out the trash, there they were, the Depends, conspicuously positioned on top of the rest of the garbage with the absorbent side up. To anyone unaware of their recent role as oil absorbers, they presented a rather unsavory sight. Naturally drawing their own conclusions, my neighbors seemed to think I was the one with a pressing need for such a large quantity of Depends. It was a misunderstanding that brought a mix of embarrassment and amusement.

Meanwhile, Maria's journey continued to intertwine with mine. She was a beacon of resilience and kindness, having moved here from the Philippines. In the months that followed her husband's passing, I assisted her with renegotiating her lease and finding her part-time work at the condo complex. Her vibrant personality and willingness to help made it easy for the complex's management to find roles that suited her skills.

I had the honor of conducting the memorial service for her husband, a man who had left his mark working at NASA. Maria's generosity knew no bounds, and in her gratitude, she presented me with NASA memorabilia, pens, coffee cups, and key rings. Each item is a tangible reminder of my time being part of her life.

However, the best gift was yet to come. Our connection continued through the years, mainly through phone calls and over coffee, where she'd update me on her life. Then, three years after her husband's death, she entrusted me with a significant role in her new beginning. Asking me to be the one to walk her down the aisle at her wedding and then take part in the ceremony.

At the wedding reception, I found the perfect moment to share the tale of the Depends, a story Maria had not heard before. The room erupted with laughter, the kind that was infectious and uncontrollable. When one guest snorted in their delight, it only added to the hilarity. The laughter was a testament to the joy of the occasion, a celebration of new beginnings, and a nod to the unexpected, often humorous paths life can take us on.

This chapter of my life, marked by my relationship with Maria and the many adventures and misadventures that came with it, was a profound reminder of the impact we can have on each other's lives. It was about more than just a chaplain's duties; it was about the human connections we forge, the laughter we share, and the memories we create, sometimes in the most unlikely circumstances.

Walking Maria down the aisle remains one of the most cherished moments of my journey as a chaplain. There was a profound sense of honor and emotional depth as I accompanied her, a symbol of a new chapter in her life. The aisle was not just a pathway in a venue but a bridge connecting past and future, sorrow and joy. Her trust in me to be part of such a pivotal moment was humbling and heartwarming.

The mystery of the excessive vitamins and supplements also eventually unraveled. In her earnest attempt to save money, it turned out that Maria had made a simple yet monumental error in her order. Thinking she was choosing the more economical option, she selected "carton" instead of "box" after entering a quantity of 144. This small checkbox mistake led to the delivery of a substantial quantity of supplements, a situation compounded by the company's refusal to accept a return. This revelation added another layer of humor and humanity to the experience.

Insights

Reflecting on these events, a couple of essential points emerged, both lighthearted and profound in their simplicity:

- Never trust a grinning firefighter with your car key. I learned this lesson amidst laughter and surprise as my Tahoe became a temporary traveling warehouse for Maria's mistaken order. While all were in good spirits, the firefighters' enjoyment of the situation was a playful reminder of the mischief that can unfold when you hand over your keys with a trustful heart.

- Beware when someone says, "Just one more thing." This phrase, often innocuous, can sometimes lead to unforeseen adventures and challenges. Maria's "one more thing" turned into a series of events that were both overwhelming and endearing. It taught me the value of patience, the importance of going with the flow, and finding humor in the unexpected.

- These experiences with Maria, the firefighters, and the community provided moments of laughter and lightheartedness. They deepened my understanding of human resilience, generosity, and the capacity to find joy in life's quirks. They were reminders that our connections with others, willingness to help, and ability to laugh at ourselves are invaluable parts of the human experience.

Reflections on the Holy Spirit

Because of the "Depends call," a stronger bond developed with the crew that responded. Laughing at an inside joke helps you become more reachable. The telling of the events of this call took on its own life as the crew enjoyed retelling the story.

Maria would not have been able to continue to live in their rented condo with the loss of income after her husband's death. Being skilled in negotiating real estate transactions provided a way to help beyond the typical role of a chaplain. Being able to help her remain in the condo and even having the condo complex realize that they could use her skills and offer her a job was a blessing to me.

I continued to talk and meet with Maria occasionally while she worked in the condo office. When she asked if I would be the one to walk her down the aisle at her wedding, it took me a minute to answer. I couldn't get the words out without tears. It remains one of my favorite memories and biggest honors.

CHAPTER 7

When Life Unravels

Start by doing what's necessary, then do what's possible and suddenly you are doing the impossible.

—Francis of Assisi

Suppose a brother or a sister is without clothes and daily food. If one of you says to them, "Go in peace; keep warm and well fed," but does nothing about their physical needs, what good is it?

—Jas 2:15–16 NIV

IN THE ANNALS OF human experience, people universally acknowledge certain events as profoundly traumatic. Among these, often cited in the top tier of life's most daunting challenges are:

- Losing a spouse
- Marriage
- Moving
- Buying a house
- Financial challenges
- Homeless

Imagine these events not as isolated incidents, but as a simultaneous surge of life-altering storms converging into one overwhelming superstorm. This torrent of turmoil can thrust the human spirit into an emotional paralysis, where feelings are no longer just muted—they're unreachable. The physical and emotional toll of such a situation is unimaginable.

My pager read:

- F 33
- UA
- Address

The resilience of the individuals I have had the honor of serving never ceases to amaze me. Faced with a whirlwind of simultaneous challenges, I can't help but wonder: Would I possess the same fortitude if I were in their shoes? It's truly a privilege to stand with them, sometimes offering guidance, support, and prayers. Their unwavering bravery and inner strength shine even on days riddled with emotional intensity and rigid circumstances.

The call was to a four-story apartment complex in Lynnwood, one of the few in the area without the convenience of an elevator. On what felt like the year's hottest day, I began the climb to the top floor in search of a thirty-three-year-old woman's residence. I found the officers in all their gear as I reached the landing. They, too, showed signs of the day's intense heat.

The lead officer introduced himself, and standing behind him was another officer who was being trained. The rookie was leaning on the railing and gazing at the parking lot. At first, it seemed he was hesitant to engage in conversation. He only shook his head then when he finally turned to face me. It was clear the call had left a mark on him. Hours later, as I stood peering over the same railing, the reason behind his response had become apparent.

When the lead officer introduced me as a chaplain, Carlos approached me, shook my hand, and immediately hugged me.

"Thank you, Father, for coming." When I heard him greet me using the title of Father, I immediately thought that he might find better comfort in the presence of a priest or a representative from his church. I offered to reach out to his church, perhaps to have a priest come by. He replied that he'd already reached out to them. They had declined to come, citing his living situation with his girlfriend before marriage as the reason.

Once I had gathered all the information about the deceased woman and spoke with the training officer, I returned to Carlos.

"Carlos, how long have you known Wendy?"

"We've dated for nearly a decade, and over the past six years, we've lived together on and off."

"On and off? What do you mean by that?"

"Wendy battled with alcohol and drugs. Things became too intense twice, and I had to ask her to leave. Witnessing her struggle was heartbreaking for me to endure. But after leaving, she sought help and went through rehab. We got back together once she was on the path to recovery. This cycle happened twice."

"I'm truly sorry to hear that. Watching a loved one grapple with addiction must've been agonizing."

"It was agonizing to see my efforts to help her fall short. Then, last year, we discovered her liver was failing."

As I entered the apartment, the stacked moving boxes instantly caught my attention, suggesting they had recently moved in. However, as Carlos delved into the story, it emerged that they weren't newcomers. They were gearing up to leave. Carlos explained they had called this apartment home for the last two years. But change was on the horizon: they had found a house to call their own and were about to leave behind the challenges of this four-story dwelling.

The mood within the apartment was somber. EMT medics were methodically packing up their equipment. In the living room, a woman, now concealed beneath a white sheet, lay as a heartbreaking symbol of the day's tragedy. It symbolized their heroic but ultimately unsuccessful efforts to save a life.

The harshness of that scene remained undisturbed for several hours until the funeral home's removal team arrived. Given the tight confines of the room, we occasionally had to step around and sometimes over her to fetch items the police needed. I worried it might seem disrespectful to Carlos.

Carlos sat at the table, responding with measured words as his emotions appeared numb. Though he spoke little, what he did share resonated. The dreams and aspirations he held for the future lay just a few feet away.

"Carlos, how long have you and Wendy been engaged?"

"Eight months. Tomorrow was going to be our wedding day." That answer stunned me. There was nothing I could think to say. Then he shared more. "We were going to have a wedding ceremony with all our friends. I don't know what to do now. I should probably start making some calls."

The reality of having your loved one die just hours before your wedding was unfathomable. I couldn't bring myself to comprehend what Carlos was experiencing. We both sat silently, reflecting on what he had just said.

I offered to help in any way I could, even with phone calls. The offer surprised him, and he asked me if I would make a few phone calls for him. When he left to get me the numbers, I stepped outside and stood by the officer-in-training, and he was still staring off into the distance. Without turning to him, I softly asked if he knew they had planned to marry the next day. He offered a quiet nod in acknowledgment before reflecting. Then, he shared, "I don't know how you can handle stuff like this, Chaplain." I did not answer.

Once back inside, Carlos told me, "I don't have everyone's phone number."

"Was Wendy planning the wedding?"

"Yes, but she had written little. It was mostly in her head."

"Do you know who was helping her?"

"Julie."

"Do you have Julie's number, and would you share it with me?"

"Thank you for doing that for me. I don't want to make that call." Then he gave me Julie's phone number.

Armed with the number, I stepped outside to make the call, sparing Carlos the added weight of overhearing. On the other end was Julie, the maid of honor and a central person in the wedding preparations alongside Wendy. Her emotions crashed when faced with the news, but her immediate inclination was to help. I quickly understood how deeply connected she was to the wedding, and she agreed to start a phone chain on Carlos's behalf, ensuring that she informed everyone involved, from attendees to the venue staff, florists, and musicians. I also requested that she keep me posted by leaving text messages.

Shortly afterward, my phone buzzed with a message from Julie. She asked me to offer Carlos her consolation and assured me she'd help with all the calls. Sharing her message on my phone with Carlos was intuitive, believing her words might bring him relief. He once more confessed his resistance to dealing with those calls himself, and upon reading Julie's text, it was clear he felt a weight lifted.

Another phone notification from Julie arrived on my phone. I opted to keep the content of this message to myself for the time being. The venue's manager had relayed his sympathies about the unfortunate turn of events, but found himself in a challenging position. Having already turned away from other potential bookings for that date, the prospect of filling the slot on such short notice seemed bleak. He based his decision to hold on to the $2,500 deposit on this, asserting it was an obligation to the venue's ownership. I hoped that if I had a personal conversation, it might provide a different outcome. I asked Julie to forward me details of the location.

With the police having departed and the funeral home's team now on-site, the apartment's atmosphere shifted. It was just Carlos, the funeral team, and me. Empathy is a tool I lean on heavily in my role, and while it often paves a path of comfort for those I'm there for, it also means I absorb a fragment of their anguish.

Over time and after countless conversations, it's become clear that my genuine concern does not go unnoticed. It signifies to the people I interact with that this is more than a mere duty to me; I genuinely care about their well being. Yet, facing Carlos's current state, the challenge was discerning tangible ways to help.

A vivid mental portrait of Carlos's ordeal began forming in my mind: the unspeakable heartbreak of losing his bride-to-be just hours before their wedding. The gravity of such a tragedy was incomprehensible to me.

Amid the heavy air, the sight of the moving boxes returned to my mind, prompting me to ask, "Carlos, could you share a bit about your planned move?"

"We'd located a home Wendy adored," he began. "Our move-in date is this Sunday."

"Just the day after tomorrow?" I clarified.

"Yes, but now that dream is dead, too." His choice of words concerned me. As he spoke of buying the house, this symbolized their shared dreams and aspirations. Yet, with the sudden loss of Wendy and the impending loss of their home, his emotions seemed to be in a state of paralysis. He was justifiably consumed by the day's events, having relinquished any hope.

Wanting to understand the scope of this new challenge, I asked, "Carlos, at what stage are you currently in the home-buying process?"

"We'd signed the closing papers yesterday. Early today, I got a call from the escrow company, telling me they expected to have the loan funded by two o'clock. But when I shared the news of Wendy's passing, they said they needed to get back to me. Shortly before you arrived, escrow called again to inform me that the lender had canceled the loan. They told me it was because Wendy was a cosigner on both the purchase and sale agreement and the loan application. Her passing away has invalidated our agreement."

Taking a moment to absorb the weight of his words, I inquired, "I assume you've already given notice here to move out?" He gave a heavy nod. "Yes, we are to be out on Sunday. The new tenant is moving in on Monday."

"Carlos, how can I pray for you?"

"I don't want our dream of buying that home to die. It may not make sense, but somehow, it would feel like I could remain connected to her in that home. Wendy and I had dreamed so much about living there and not in an apartment anymore. We have been together for ten years, and it was finally going to happen on Sunday."

Witnessing the extent of broken dreams that Carlos faced in just a matter of hours was heart wrenching. Surprisingly, he bore it all with a stoic calm, devoid of the outward emotions you might expect.

"Carlos, if there was even a glimmer of a possibility for you to continue to buy the home, would you want to consider it? Or is its weight too overwhelming at this moment?"

Carlos looked up, his voice laced with defeat. "Father, I can't envision a way forward. It seems like a lost cause now after speaking with the lender."

I hesitated, handpicking my words, feeling it was important that my primary profession outside of chaplaincy didn't diminish the trust he had already placed in me.

"The Lord has a way of equipping us all with unique talents. Perhaps some of mine might be of use here."

He looked at me, curious. "What do you mean?"

"I serve as a chaplain on a volunteer basis, serving two days a week in this ministry. But my primary profession is as a real estate broker. If you allow me, I might be able to help."

He slowly nodded. "I don't know how, but sure."

"Could I look at the paperwork related to the house purchase?" He located the file on the kitchen counter and passed it to me. "With your permission, I'd like to make a few calls on your behalf. I'll keep it on speaker, ensuring you hear the conversations."

Carlos, still skeptical, murmured, "I'm not sure they'll reconsider soon enough to make a difference."

It was about 2:00 p.m. when I first contacted the lender with some specific questions. Is Wendy's income needed to qualify for the loan? The answer was that it was helpful, but not required. The lender immediately understood where I was going. He said he wanted to crunch some numbers and would call me back.

He called back thirty minutes later after speaking to the loan underwriters. If Carlos could redo the paperwork and get it back to him on Monday, he could have the loan rewritten and ready again by Thursday to be re-signed. However, he pointed out that the agreement has expired. The seller also needed to agree to extend the sale. Home prices were going up fast, and the home was now worth much more than the agreed price.

Following that conversation, I called the agent who was representing Carlos. I gave him an overview and told him I had already received a positive response from the lender. However, I would like to talk to the listing agent directly. He knew of my reputation in the local real estate community and reluctantly agreed. The next call was to the listing agent. I explained what had happened, and he wanted to confirm the financing details personally with Carlos's lender. Once he had confirmed everything with the lender, he called back. He was okay with what we were trying to do. He would now call the seller.

"Would it be possible for me to talk to the seller?" Hesitating, he agreed, if I would call him back after I spoke with him. Then he said he would follow up. These conversations had all been on the speaker. I could see some hope developing in Carlos's eyes. Using my expertise to assist him in this way was a privilege. Between the calls, Carlos agreed to pause and pray with me.

Reaching out to the seller, I introduced myself as a chaplain. I sensed hesitation in his voice. We later discovered he had been close to hanging up, thinking it was some scam caller. It took a few minutes to answer his questions, reassure him about who I was and why I was calling, and address his concerns. But he was very understanding about Carlos's situation. The two of them talked for a few minutes, and it came out that the seller had lost his wife four years ago. He graciously agreed to extend the closing time and redo the papers at the same price so the sale could go through.

Learning the house was vacant, I asked the seller for one more favor. Carlos did not know what I had on my mind and looked puzzled. The favor asked was if the seller would allow Carlos to move in on Sunday as planned, sharing that Carlos had already reserved a moving van and had friends coming to help with the move. People rarely consider early possession because it takes months to evict a tenant when things go wrong. That was why I wanted to speak with the seller directly. Brokers advise sellers not to consider this; however, if they allow early possession, they require the buyer to pay a deposit and rent as compensation.

In anticipation of this, I offered to pay whatever rent the seller might want personally until the sale closed, if he would consider it. It was my way of letting him know I was considering how this affected him. After a prolonged silence on the phone, the seller finally responded with a resolute "No!" Observing Carlos, I saw the disappointment cross his face, his hopes visibly deflating. Yet, after another brief pause, the seller's tone shifted. "I don't want you to pay any rent or deposit. Give me your address, and I'll bring the keys over in twenty minutes."

I wanted to make sure that Carlos had space to grieve the loss of his fiancée. However, all these other distractions were too much for anyone to handle. He was so overwhelmed with everything coming at him he couldn't deal with Wendy's loss.

Sometimes, life can bring profound devastation. Losing Wendy, the void of a wedding that would never be, and the subsequent loss of their shared dream of their own home painted a clear picture of Carlos's burdens. I thought it was no wonder he appeared so stoically affected, recounting what he was up against:

- He was to be married in less than twenty-four hours.
- His fiancée had died.
- Escrow told him that the loan would not close now.
- Being unable to close on time, his earnest money was at risk.
- The lender rescinded the loan.
- He still had to make heartbreaking calls to those coming to the wedding.
- He was losing the deposit for the wedding location.
- On top of that, in two days, he would be homeless, with nowhere to go, but he still had to be out of his apartment by Sunday evening.

Now, adding to those:

- Planning a memorial service
- Search for a place new to live

With everything taken care of for the home purchase, I sat down with Carlos and talked about Wendy. He shared some stories and built an image of who she was. Hesitating, he also shared with me her problems with alcohol addiction and what he had experienced watching her struggle with trying to overcome it.

As I exited the apartment and gently closed the door, I gravitated to the railing where the police officers had stood earlier. Now, it was I who stared distantly, lost in thought. Witnessing someone undergo such a barrage of life-altering events in rapid succession is profoundly unsettling. And as I stood there, lost in reflection, a persistent sense of unease still gripped me.

I went back to the door and knocked. Carlos opened the door, and we looked at each other without speaking. Then I opened my arms, and he quickly came forward, hanging on to me and sobbing. We stood outside his door for several minutes, then returned inside and he shared more. He now grieved for Wendy. He shared how proud he was of her for being a fighter and not giving up or letting drugs or alcohol get the best of her.

On Tuesday, I visited Carlos at his new home and found him unpacking. Tentatively, I asked how he was holding up. While the question always felt somewhat inadequate, I trusted Carlos would recognize the genuine concern behind it, knowing I was truly there to listen. A few moments into our conversation, I presented Carlos with an envelope. The wedding venue owners had entrusted it to me after we met in person. They asked if I would deliver it to him.

A check fell out as Carlos opened the condolence card envelope to read the owner's handwritten note. Picking it up, he found it was a full refund of his deposit.

To me, this was witnessing God in action. As I observed how he orchestrated all the significant and minute details, I felt again that I had the privilege of witnessing God in action from a front-row seat.

Insights

- Drawing from countless calls, I understood the immense challenge of making phone calls after distressing events. Delving into painful details often requires sharing more than one might feel prepared to, alongside navigating a barrage of probing questions.
- I learned the value of pausing briefly before making any phone calls. The suggestion to wait until after speaking with the first responders

offered people a much-needed moment to collect their thoughts and emotions.

- One call affecting people most was to funeral homes. The terminology and questions they ask are often not sensitive. Removal, unfortunately, is one term used, and questions about the deceased person's weight become uncomfortable to answer. If they wanted me to make the calls, I would step outside or away from the family so they wouldn't hear. They seemed to always express their appreciation.

- I observed that a brief pause could significantly ease the burden of the tough conversations. I offered further support to those who seemed unsure about what to say, helping script their words. These suggestions aimed to guide them through the challenging dialogues, making the process less daunting.

Reflections on the Holy Spirit

There are moments when an inner certainty tells you that you are precisely where you should be. The five chaplains in our organization each come with our unique blend of life experiences, education, and personal reasons for wanting to serve. My journey as a real estate broker into chaplaincy uniquely equipped me for this call. The reputation I had built with lenders and agents within our community now opened doors for Carlos, allowing a direct conversation with the underwriter and the seller.

After leaving Carlos's apartment for the first time, I paused at the railing, lost in thought, as I stared into the distance. The events that had just unfolded left me with an unsettled feeling, compelling me to return and knock on his door once more. When Carlos opened the door and embraced me, he began to mourn for Wendy. As we stepped back inside, I was profoundly glad I hadn't walked away, leaving him to face his sorrow alone this day. I give the Holy Spirit credit for all.

CHAPTER 8

How Could a Used Paperback Novel Change a Child's Life?

Learn to light a candle in the darkest moments of someone's life. Be the light that helps others see; it is what gives life its deepest significance.

—Roy T. Bennett, *The Light in the Heart*

From a young age, life dealt me its fair share of heartbreaks. I faced the devastating loss of my father at just nine years old, and by twenty-two, I had to say goodbye to my mother. Those trials during my early years enriched me with deep-seated empathy. This has helped me intimately understand the profound grief of losing a parent at a young age: the quiet longings, treasured memories, and perpetual reflections of missed life lessons.

My pager read:

- F 34
- UA
- Address

The link between the painting and the story from the mystery novel was marginal. To this day, it amazes me how the Holy Spirit combined the two to craft a suggestion that left a profound mark on a young boy.

Before sharing about Trevor and Maggie, I want to shed light on the source of my help for this call. I'm convinced that the Holy Spirit directed my gaze to a small painting near the front door as I entered. As the day unfolded and my conversation with Trevor's dad deepened, the significance of the piece of art grew. It stirred memories of a vacation trip and then down a convoluted trail to a discarded novel I read.

When I mention to others that a book with an explanation about listening inspired me, the conversation often takes a predictable turn. Some people try to guess the title, while others offer Bible verses emphasizing the power of listening. Interestingly, the guesses are more logical than the true source of my inspiration: Tony Hillerman's *The Blessing Way*.

The book I'm referring to wasn't a profound spiritual work, an enlightening reference, or a guide for counseling. It was a mystery novel, a light read for beach lounging. Think of it like those glossy magazines we flip through in a waiting room, even if we have little interest in the latest celebrity fashion, "Who Wore It Better."

This occurred years before I took on the role of a chaplain. We were camping at Lookout State Park in Oregon, stretching our legs after two days on the road. My suspicion about what I call "Camper Chronicles" is they're books that couldn't find a home at a used bookstore, so they're left behind. Not to pass on something of value to another traveler, just freeing up space. This time, the book rescued me from rereading the golf magazines and other books I had finished earlier.

I found consolation in immersing myself in those pages, glancing up to watch the rhythmic crashing of waves and the graceful soaring of seagulls and pelicans. Meanwhile, my wife had her ritual of scouring the coastline for sand dollars and various sea gems. There's this inexplicable urge she has to gift these marine treasures to our grandkids. Given that we have five grandkids, her collection grew. On this occasion, I discovered her assortment of prizes not by sight but by a recognizable scent, enhanced by the heat of the day and the hundred and seventy miles we covered later that afternoon. This sensory recollection brought forth memories, especially those tied to a foundational figure in most of our lives: our mother.

The title *mother* is one of the most revered and significant. A mother's love is steadfast, and her roles are diverse. She is a caregiver, confidant, chef, coach, nurse, and teacher, each executed with an unparalleled heart and dedication. Every child sees their mother as an irreplaceable pillar of strength and compassion. While, as adults, we understand the depth of her love for children, we often realize the enormity of a mother's absence during poignant moments later in life.

Losing a mother is an agonizing ordeal that doesn't discriminate across cultures or ages. Although it's a part of life's cycle, the anguish remains intense. Such grief will profoundly affect a child, changing their world. Calls involving young children who have lost a parent strike a profound chord within me. Seeing the unfiltered grief and confusion in their eyes is a poignant reminder of life's delicate nature and the deep bonds we share.

The call came on Thursday at 07:30 a.m.

It was a call concerning a young mother named Terri. Though I was still in the early stages of my chaplaincy, I trusted that the Holy Spirit would always guide me, offering the insights necessary to connect with those at the scenes. This belief ensured I never felt isolated or unaided during my calls.

When I got out of my car, two local police officers explained the situation and introduced me to Terri's children: twelve-year-old Maggie and nine-year-old Trevor. They also mentioned that Terri's ex-husband and the medical examiner were en route, but wouldn't arrive for another hour. To ensure I grasped the circumstances, one officer led me to the distressing scene the children had faced just thirty minutes earlier.

The sight was disturbing: Terri's face had turned a deep shade of purple, her eyes frozen in an expression of pain. Although her face was now covered by a sheet, the haunting image could linger in the children's minds for a long time.

It's painful to think of the enduring impact that an experience like this can have. Traumatic visuals, especially for children, can leave indelible imprints on the mind. It's heart wrenching to think of how these memories might influence their emotions in the future. My goal is to find ways to replace the visual image and not let it become embedded in their memory as quickly as possible.

During our conversation, I couldn't help but notice Maggie and Trevor's frequent glances toward the door that separated them from their mother. It took a while to gain Maggie's trust; then after a gentle nudge, Maggie began to open up, reminiscing about cherished moments with their mom. Her voice filled with warmth as she shared about their favorite hikes and the movie nights together. The family room's bookshelves overflowed with countless VCR tapes and DVDs, each one a memory of their time spent together. Although Maggie shared, Trevor seemed lost in his thoughts and chose silence as his hiding place.

As they grew more at ease with my presence, I inquired if they had any recent photographs of their mother they'd be willing to show me. They left and soon returned, each bearing a small collection of photos. I wondered if there was a particular image they both cherished. Without hesitation, they pointed to the same photograph. It captured the trio, radiant smiles on their faces, with the majestic backdrop of a cascading waterfall. Maggie recounted the story of their recent escapade to Wallace Falls, a day of adventure and laughter.

Our conversation flowed, and sensing an opportune moment, I inquired, "Do you believe your mom would want you to cherish her memory through the joyous moments, like those captured in this photograph, rather than how you discovered her?" Their heads tilted in somber acknowledgment. I gently continued, "Whenever grief washes over, or you revisit how your mom looked when you found her, perhaps you could view this photo from Wallace Falls. Let this moment of joy become your memory." In the following hours, I saw them repeatedly glance at the treasured image.

Trevor had been notably quiet since I arrived, speaking only with his sister when they were by themselves.

His father joined us after an hour and a half; during the wait, Trevor had continued to be quiet except for a few moments. His dad remarked that it wasn't uncommon for Trevor to remain withdrawn. Then, their father took a moment to explain more about Trevor. He mentioned that, while Trevor might not always be the most vocal in a room, he had this innate ability to observe and reflect. When he shared his insights, they were deep and strikingly insightful. As we continued the conversation, Trevor stood right there beside us. I couldn't help but feel discomfort. It was as though we were discussing a painting in a gallery while the artist stood by, unnoticed, making the whole interaction feel somewhat awkward.

It brought to mind a chat I had with my son regarding the personalities he sometimes hired. I shared that he had observed that those who remained quiet often had the most valuable insights during and after meetings. Their knack for listening without dominating the conversation made them invaluable assets to his teams. These quieter individuals grasp the broader perspective, unlike those who are preoccupied with formulating their next statement. As I spoke with the father, my mind went back to the painting hanging in the entryway.

Upon entering the home, Navajo artwork adorning the walls drew my attention for some unknown reason. A particular painting near the front door depicting Kokopelli captivated me even before I met the children. Hearing Trevor's dad apologize for him, that image resurfaced in my thoughts. I felt a growing urge to advocate for Trevor in his father's eyes, and an idea crystallized on how I might offer insight that might change his perspective.

So I asked the father if I could show him and Trevor something important. Once we were in front of the art, I told them the name of the figure in the painting, Kokopelli, and that it was Navajo. I explained that one of the Navajo's well-known qualities is their ability to listen without interruption or voicing opinions. In conversations with Navajos, most individuals find the long silence after telling a story or expressing an idea disconcerting. Most outsiders feel uncomfortable and think that the Navajo people missed the point of what was said and are unsure of how to react.

However, the long silence is a courtesy that the Navajo provides. They give you time to see if you want to change or add anything or continue with whatever your thoughts are. Once you get used to the silence, it can change how you process the conversation. This information came to me from the paperback novel by Tony Hillerman that I had read years before. I could never have imagined that the book would be helpful for anything. With a calm and reassuring tone, I explained to Kevin that his son possessed the rare gift of patient listening, which might introduce fresh insights into discussions.

What happened next astonished both of us. Trevor started talking and went on for about ten minutes, explaining what he had seen today and how he was processing it. Before I left, Kevin told me he never remembered his son sharing like that.

Memorial Service

Weeks after Terri's passing, I had the privilege of speaking at her memorial service. In preparation, I spent time with Kevin and their children, delving deeper into understanding who Terri was. They shared that Terri's work included supporting and counseling battered and at-risk women who lived in a designated apartment building nearby. During a visit, Trevor's dad confided in me, expressing his newfound ability to slow down and remain calm while conversing with his son. He admired his son's impressive thought process and wished he had been more patient with him before.

To prepare for the memorial, I visited her office and had meaningful conversations with a few of the women she had been guiding. They all recounted stories of Terri's boundless compassion and influence on their lives. Drawing from my own experiences, I suggested how impactful it would be for her children if they could pen a note or share these stories, further explaining that "her children knew her as mom, but hearing your accounts could provide a fuller understanding of their mother, creating a lasting legacy of her life."

I stayed in touch with the family for a few years afterward. Trevor's dad told me he had become more comfortable speaking now, which was a cherished gift to me.

Chaplaincy has taught me to ensure that I see what is often right in front of me, trying to gain some awareness about a family. Every response has its own one-of-a-kind quality. Personalities, circumstances, and backgrounds never repeat. Even with excellent training, you must adapt as soon as you arrive.

Insights

- [1]Losing a parent during your formative years leaves a lasting gap. The what ifs and thoughts of what might have been persist for the rest of your life. Memories of them become essential touchstones. Hearing stories or memories from others about your parents can provide a fuller, richer understanding of their lives.

- Images from traumatic events linger in our minds. We can try to forget them, but memories hold on to strong visuals. With children, these impressions are even more pronounced. Their still-maturing minds and developing emotional defenses makes them more susceptible. Having limited life experiences intensifies their reactions to such events. I also believe external influences, like the graphic content in movies and media, play into their understanding of trauma.

- Photographs are the timeless witnesses of moments passed, silent yet eloquent relics that offer us a window to look back through time. In each frame, they capture not just faces, but feelings, stories, and a connection that death cannot sever. They serve as a comforting reminder

1. For more on how children grieve see appendix. See also beyondthesirens.com.

that once, in a moment captured forever, everything was perfect. I do not know where the idea of using photos to replace the last sight of their mother's face came from.

- My training for becoming a chaplain began at age nine. Early on, life dealt me its fair share of heartbreaks. I faced the devastating loss of my father at just nine years old, and by twenty-two, I had to say goodbye to my mother. Ever since those events, the moments I share with my brother often lead us to ponder the paths our lives might have taken had they been beside us. Yet, when we encounter a surprise, a story, or an unknown detail about our parents, we cherish them. These rare and precious moments carry a weight of significance that I understand all too well. Those trials during my formative years enriched me with deep-seated empathy. This has helped me understand the profound grief of losing a parent at a young age: the quiet longings, treasured memories, and perpetual reflections of missed life lessons.

- [2]More about the Navajo way of listening.

Reflections on the Holy Spirit

Reflecting on the Holy Spirit's role, the news of children aged nine and eleven experiencing the loss of a parent in this call moved me. It brought back memories of losing my father. I realized that my past loss was preparing me to help others in unexpected ways.

The book I stumbled upon was in terrible condition. After putting it down for the third time, I almost didn't take it. Sand fell from it, the cover was almost off, and some pages were loose. Yet this worn-out book enabled Trevor to find his voice and gain confidence.

My confidence in speaking with the authority to assist the father stemmed from my understanding that my life experiences had already equipped me for this moment.

If I were on standby, my phone and pager would go off when needed. I seldom knew anything about the volatile situation I would walk into or what the authorities needed until I arrived on the scene, but that was okay. Serving as a chaplain was an excellent exercise for my prayer life. Given

---

2. For more about the Navajo way of listening see appendix. See also beyondthesirens.com.

the multitude of answered prayers I had encountered, I had an unwavering belief that HE would always be there.

Invitation to the Reader

If you feel empathy for the families and individuals in these encounters, consider looking into serving as a chaplain. There are many opportunities and ways to serve.

You may also discover that because of your personal history and your gifts, there will be times when you are sure you were supposed to be the chaplain to respond. This was one of them for me.

CHAPTER 9

Forever Young: Taylor's Legacy

If ever there is a tomorrow when we're not together—there is something you must always remember. You are braver than you believe, stronger than you seem, and smarter than you think. But the most important thing is, even if we're apart—I'll always be with you.

—A. A. MILNE, *WINNIE THE POOH*

THEY SAY TIME IS a thief, but there are moments in life when our memory of someone seems to pause, and they remain forever young.

My pager read:

- F9
- CPR
- Address

Now serving as the lead chaplain for our fire district, I mentored new chaplains, including Aaron, a pastor and a recent addition to the team. With the support of his congregation and his own wise, empathetic, and compassionate approach, Aaron was a valuable asset to the team. He had shown a knack for handling various challenges, reducing the need for my oversight in familiar situations.

The police had requested a chaplain for an incident involving a nine-year-old girl, and Aaron, who was on call that Thursday, was asked to respond. Since the location was only a few minutes away, it was a chance to observe how he would handle such a delicate situation.

Arriving fifteen minutes after the dispatch, I stayed back, blending in with gathered neighbors as I tried to find Aaron amidst the crowded scene of first responders and their vehicles.

In the chaos, an officer unexpectedly recognized me and approached. First, he offered reassurance about Aaron's competent handling of the situation. However, he also hinted at the complex family dynamics in play, suggesting my experience might help navigate these additional layers.

Below is information on the people involved:

- Taylor—a nine-year-old girl
- Parker—Taylor's younger brother, a five-year-old with profound autism who does not understand the situation
- Ray—their father, who also is on the spectrum
- Jessica—Ray's ex-wife and Taylor and Parker's mother
- Sally—Ray's mother
- Carolyn—Jessica's mother
- Michael—Jessica's new husband
- Two black dogs—one about sixty pounds, the other about thirty pounds
- Three police officers
- Fire department safety officer—required on calls like this
- The fire department's usual response team—a ladder truck, two firefighters, and a medic unit
- Jennifer—the medical examiner
- Aaron—a pastor who also served as chaplain for this call

I returned to my car to retrieve my coat to allow me more freedom to move around the scene. Returning, a police officer urgently directed me inside. He learned from a firefighter that they were expecting the call to end resuscitative efforts and required a chaplain inside *now* for the father's support.

Seeing Aaron already engrossed in an emotional conversation with one grandmother outside, I waved at him to let him know I was there, then entered the home. Inside, the atmosphere was intense. Ray, the other grandmother, three police officers, the fire department safety officer, and two standby medics were all singularly focused on the CPR team's efforts. Each compression was a collective moment of hope, and I observed a unique phenomenon: those not directly involved in the action were unconsciously swaying in sync with the rhythm of each compression.

The atmosphere in the room drastically changed when the doctor gave the order to stop the CPR efforts and announced the time of death at 2:17 p.m. Ray inadvertently overheard the heartbreaking news. He reacted instantly, screaming as he dashed out of the room. A medic, catching my eye, conveyed his regret about how the father learned of his daughter's passing.

I searched for Ray, checking the main bedroom and backyard, but found no sign of him. Searching downstairs, a sound I did not recognize and had never heard before led me to him. Initially, it seemed like a trapped dog, but I realized it was Ray, locked in the bathroom, when I felt the walls tremble from his desperate pounding.

Feeling lost for what to say or do, I fetched several water bottles from the ladder truck and set them outside the bathroom door. Knocking gently, I informed him about the water and encouraged him to take his time. When he emerged to take the bottles, he questioned what would happen next. After introducing myself as the chaplain and answering his questions, I explained that there was nothing he needed to do now, and I also understood his need for solitude. "Ray, if you want to remain here, I will keep everyone away until you are ready to come out." Leaving him, I went upstairs to find Aaron.

As we exchanged perspectives and information in the living room, a woman's urgent voice interrupted our conversation, calling out, "No, no, Parker, no. You need to play outside for now."

At that moment, Parker burst into the room. His laughter and energy, so full of life, starkly contrasted with the somberness of our surroundings. He seemed oblivious to the gravity of the situation, innocently jumping over his sister's body. Close on his heels were the two dogs, adding to the hectic energy. Chasing them was the woman we'd heard outside. She appeared overwhelmed, trying vainly to herd Parker and the dogs back out of the room.

Parker continued his impromptu game a few more times, weaving around the room before finally darting out the door he had come in. The dogs, barking excitedly, followed in hot pursuit, with the woman's frantic calls of NO! echoing behind them.

Aaron and I exchanged glances, momentarily lost in the surreal nature of what we had just witnessed. The room's atmosphere blended with chaos and grief, a poignant reminder of the tragedy that had unfolded here.

Another disturbance soon followed this brief, bizarre interlude. Two older women, one of them the woman who had been chasing Parker and the dogs, entered the room, each visibly distraught. They moved with purpose, each trying to get closer to the deceased girl. The police responded quickly, gently guiding one woman outside. When the officer returned, he approached Aaron and me with an explanation. He identified the women as the girl's grandmothers: Carolyn, her maternal grandmother and Parker's pursuer, and Sally, Ray's mother. Both were understandably upset, and the tension between them had escalated.

Recognizing the situation's sensitivity, Aaron went to speak with Carolyn while I approached Sally, who had stepped outside. She was pacing on the sidewalk and her unease was apparent in her movements. Sally strongly desired to be with her son, but I understood that doing so might create complications with the police. I gently explained the situation to her, assuring her we were focused on her son's well being. Her response was a mix of concern and frustration.

"You have no idea what he's dealing with," Sally said, her voice tinged with sorrow and exasperation.

I nodded in understanding, recognizing the truth in her words. "You're right, Sally. Could you tell me what you think I need to know to support him better?" I invited her to help me understand their family's unique challenges.

In a series of revealing details, Sally shared with me the intricate fabric of their family life over the past year. She spoke of her son, Ray, who is on the higher-functioning end of the autism spectrum. This aspect of Ray's life brought unique daily challenges, shaping his interactions and experiences. In a similar vein, she talked about her grandson, Parker, also high on the spectrum, whose needs for care and attention were constant and specific. Observing Parker's behavior, I noticed his perception of the world was different. His playful engagement with Carolyn, who often looked after him, was a routine that provided him comfort and a sense of normalcy. His playing chase was a regular part of his world, and the day's tragic events seemed distant from his immediate reality.

Sally's tone changed as she delved deeper into Ray's story, marked by significant trials and tribulations. Two years ago, doctors diagnosed him with stage four cancer, and he has since faced grueling treatments and bleak prognoses. The journey was physically and emotionally taxing, involving aggressive chemotherapy and a bone marrow transplant. Amidst this struggle for survival, Ray faced a personal upheaval. Jessica, now his ex-wife, rekindled a relationship with a high school sweetheart through Facebook, leading to her eventual departure from their marriage. The day Ray returned from a chemotherapy session was the day he received divorce papers, a moment that marked a painful turning point in his life. Jessica later married her old flame, Michael, and moved to Port Townsend, Washington, a location not easily accessible, involving a two-hour journey and catching a ferry.

Initially, Sally found it challenging to maintain civility toward Carolyn, Jessica's mother, especially given the circumstances under which her daughter left Ray. However, as time passed, she observed Carolyn's unwavering commitment to caring for Parker, Taylor, and even Ray. This observation gradually transformed Sally's view of Carolyn, fostering a begrudging respect for her dedication and love.

Before returning to the house, I asked Sally for a moment alone. I needed to talk with Ray first, and it also gave me the time to process everything Sally had shared. The intricate details of a family grappling with such profound challenges were a lot to take in.

The thought struck me as I stood by my car. I hoped to convey to Ray that his daughter's life and her time in the world mattered. However, meeting this family for the first time today posed a question: How could I effectively communicate this?

After reentering the house, I approached the bathroom door where Ray was. Tapping lightly, I asked if he felt ready to step out. The moment I saw his face, the depth of his grief was tangible in his expression, rendering words excessive. In a spontaneous gesture, I embraced him, and he reciprocated with equal intensity. It was a moment where words were unnecessary. Gently, I informed him that his mother, Sally, was outside, her presence potentially a source of comfort. Watching mother and son reunite, I stepped away to find Aaron.

I found Aaron in the living room amidst the firefighters and police officers, all sharing information about the unfolding situation. Aaron and I moved to the kitchen for a more private conversation. He needed to know what I learned about the relationships and the autism. There was a high probability that Sally had been protective of her son most of his life and might attempt to take over today.

Aaron relayed his conversation with Carolyn, who was eager to help. I shared that Sally had been a pillar of protection for her son his entire life, understandable when considering his autism. This protective stance had sometimes led to friction with Carolyn, particularly during the tumultuous period of Ray's cancer treatment and the ensuing divorce.

However, Sally's perspective developed, notably when she witnessed Carolyn's unwavering care for Taylor, Parker, and even Ray. On this day, Aaron had skillfully kept Carolyn, Parker, and the dogs engaged in the backyard, maintaining a semblance of normalcy amidst the crisis.

Our focus then shifted to the room where Taylor lay. Her body, covered only by a plain white sheet on the hard floor, presented a harsh and impersonal image. Aaron and I both felt an immediate need to change this. We found a blanket adorned with pastel-colored animal illustrations and a soft pink pillow in her room. These items, though simple, had the potential to transform the setting. Draping the blanket over Taylor and placing the pillow under her head infused the space with warmth and dignity.

As Aaron and I fully understood the extent of Ray's struggles, we grappled with how best to pay tribute to Taylor's life. The strange thing was we were not sure why this desire was so strong in us. We knew nothing about Taylor's life, but we both felt it. Yet, discovering the most fitting way to convey this would be challenging.

Once outside, I joined Ray and Sally, and she was eager to see Taylor. Her sense of urgency, a reflection of her deep involvement in the family's affairs, was unmistakable. However, the circumstances required a delicate touch. With as much empathy as I could muster, I gently explained to her the necessity of waiting for the medical examiner's clearance, emphasizing the importance of balancing procedural requirements with the family's emotional needs. However, this part of my role often left me feeling like I was being unkind to the families. From their perspective, it would seem rules intended to preserve a crime scene overshadowed their needs, especially when three officers stood just five feet away, seemingly already enforcing this priority.

Noticing an opportune moment for a private conversation, I suggested a short walk with Ray. We needed to discuss Jessica in a setting away from the ears of Sally. "Ray, have you considered calling Jessica?" I asked, gently broaching the subject. Ray hesitated. "What should I say? She's in Port Townsend," he began. The distance compounded the problem. I advised him to keep it simple and urgent to prompt her to come without revealing too much. "She needs to know it's important, Ray. Also, ask her to text you once she's on the ferry so we can be ready for her." The thought behind this was to reduce Ray's options.

When Ray wondered about handling Jessica's questions, I offered a straightforward solution: "Just tell her you need her here as soon as possible and then hang up." I could see the weight of the situation on his shoulders and offered further support. "This might be kinder for Jessica, not knowing everything during the long drive. Do you want me to ask your mom to make the call instead?" He considered for a moment and then handled it himself.

After Ray made the call, Jessica called back a few times. However, based on my advice, these calls went unanswered since Ray was not at a place where he could answer all the questions Jessica would have. I hoped it would lead to a safer, more controlled journey for Jessica and Michael if they did not fully realize the extent of the tragedy.

I found Aaron engaged in a quiet conversation with the three officers, positioned a few feet away from where Taylor lay. He later shared with me that their discussion was brief and deliberately light, focusing on topics like their shift experiences and fishing, a conscious effort to steer clear of the somber reality before them. The only exception was their reaction to an unexpected moment when Parker, accompanied by the dogs, suddenly reentered the room. His playful antics, innocently leaping over his sister, momentarily disrupted the solemnity, briefly turning the mournful quiet into a scene of chaos.

Jennifer, the medical examiner, arrived and, with compassion, immediately began her detailed investigation. She moved efficiently, taking photographs and talking with the officers, and her professionalism was clear in every action. As she wrapped up her tasks and had a brief yet significant conversation with Ray, Ray received a crucial update via text: Jessica was now on the ferry, roughly forty minutes from reaching us.

I took this moment to approach Jennifer, requesting a favor. Could we possibly keep Taylor here, as she was for a little longer, foregoing the immediate use of a body bag to allow Jessica a chance to see her daughter when she arrived? Understanding the emotional weight of this request, Jennifer agreed sympathetically, acknowledging the importance of these last moments for the grieving family. It would do more than bring some sense of closure to Jessica; It would help her immensely in the days ahead.

During the waiting period, Ray, Sally, and Carolyn huddled together, embarking on a journey down memory lane, sharing heartfelt stories about Taylor. They reminisced about her vibrant life, particularly her remarkable connections at school. Their shared stories painted a picture of a girl deeply loved and admired by her peers and teachers. Her kindness, her eagerness to help others, and her active participation in school activities were themes that resonated in every story. Listening to these stories, Ray's love for his daughter was visible, and his face conveyed both sorrow and pride. These stories touched me deeply, igniting the desire within me to honor Taylor's legacy further. Amidst the stories, playful mentions of Taylor being the unspoken favorite of the teacher lightened the mood, bringing brief smiles in a time of grief.

The moment of waiting ended when Ray noticed Jessica's car parked at the end of the street. A sense of urgency overtook him, his hand gripping my arm tightly. His voice, shaky with nerves, betrayed his uncertainty. "What should I say to her?" he asked me. I advised, "Tell her Taylor has died, Ray. She needs to know, and then she'll need time to process it."

As we approached the car, Jessica stepped out, confusion etched on her face, accompanied by her new husband, Michael. Seeing all the police cars, she asked, "What's happening?" her voice laced with worry. Almost instinctively, Ray faced me, his eyes imploring, "You tell her," asking me to be the one to deliver the news. As I stood beside Jessica, with Michael standing silently close to her, I delivered the tragic news with as much gentleness as I could muster. "Jessica, there's been an emergency. Taylor collapsed, and Ray immediately called 911. The medics did everything in their power to revive her, but I'm so sorry, they couldn't save her. Taylor has passed away."

Over my years of service, I have seen a spectrum of reactions to such news. Some lashed out, others withdrew, each person's grief manifesting differently. Being the messenger, I often felt a pang of guilt in those moments, as if I were partly responsible for their pain.

Jessica's reaction was immediate and spontaneous. Her knees buckled under the weight of the news, and Ray and I instinctively reached out to steady her. Michael quickly came to her aid, providing a steady shoulder for her to lean on. Through her tears, she expressed an urgent desire to see Taylor, and we guided her back toward the house.

We wanted to give Taylor's family a private moment with her before the arduous task of preparing her for the transportation. Knowing the deep sorrow this moment brings, I talked with Sally and Ray outside, questioning if Carolyn could be part of the last goodbye. Carolyn's empathy shone through, and it was clear Sally felt Carolyn's presence was vital during this intensely personal time.

Nearby, the three police officers stood in a solemn vigil, their arms folded, gripping the tops of their protective vests. This silent respect and readiness posture had been the same since my arrival. However, I observed there was a noticeable lack of conversation among them. Aaron also stood by the family while a neighbor was outside, distracting Parker and the dogs.

Once inside, Jessica moved quickly, her maternal instinct drawing her to Taylor's side. Ray, caught up in the moment and wanting me to be near her, deliberately pushed me forward, causing a collision with an officer. The sergeant observed this minor commotion and offered a simple thumbs-up that only I could see. It surprised me how much that silent message meant to me, encouraging my efforts.

The medical examiner let us know it was time, and kindly asked the family to step outside. The process of wrapping a body and placing it into a bag can deeply imprint on the memories of families, becoming a vivid recollection. As she prepared to wrap Taylor in the plastic sheet, there was an unforeseen obstacle: the medical examiner found the task challenging. Unexpectedly, the police officers, typically prompt to step in and help, stood by without moving.

Without being asked, Aaron and I stepped forward. Though we had performed this task before, this situation felt singularly emotional as the medical examiner stepped back, leaving us responsible. We tenderly wrapped Taylor and placed her in the bag, but instead of waiting for a gurney, we carried her out ourselves, a gesture of care and respect.

Later, at another call, one officer sought me out to apologize for his inaction. He explained that his daughter was the same age and the task was too overwhelming.

A heavy sense of introspection enveloped me as Aaron and I parted ways. Despite effort, I wrestled with the feeling that I hadn't reasonably conveyed to the family the full significance of Taylor's life. The question of how to honor Taylor meaningfully in a way that genuinely mirrored the impact she had made weighed heavily on my mind. Despite the challenge of never meeting Taylor and knowing very little about her, I desired to honor her on behalf of her family. I wanted to find a tangible way to create a lasting tribute to provide a perpetual memory of her. I questioned if I was being realistic.

Five Days Later

It was the following Tuesday, and my wife and I were coleading a small Bible study group with Clarence, a third-grade teacher, and his wife in their home. After finishing our lesson, we transitioned into a time of sharing prayer requests. When it was Clarence's turn, he struggled to articulate his words, his eyes downcast. He revealed that a third-grade student, his favorite, had tragically passed away the week before. His request for prayers for the bereaved family was heartfelt, and he expressed a deep-seated wish to support them, although regulations prevented him from making direct contact. Another group member asked for the girl's first name to be included in their prayers. Before Clarence could respond, I uttered, "Taylor." Our eyes met, and a silent acknowledgment passed between us with the realization I had been part of that heart-wrenching call. Tears formed in both of our eyes, reflecting the shared tragedy.

As the evening drew to a close, Clarence and I took a moment to discuss ways we might honor Taylor's memory. He was hopeful about establishing a memorial in the school library, a sentiment echoed by other teachers. However, when they proposed this idea to the principal, they encountered a bureaucratic wall: the school district did not permit student memorials. Undeterred, Clarence still yearned to express his feelings to Taylor's family and inquired if I could facilitate a meeting with her father.

Given that Ray's mother had stipulated that all communication with Ray should go through her, I approached the situation sensitively. I scheduled a meeting with her three days later. Although I was there at the conference, Clarence steered the conversation. Initially, uncertainty hung in the air, but everything changed when Clarence revealed a note from Taylor. It was a simple message expressing her gratitude for how he always reserved her favorite books just for her. This small yet profound token illuminated how Taylor's spirit continued to resonate through the fond memories her teachers treasured. For Sally, it was an emotional realization of Taylor's lasting imprint at her school, a testament to her enduring impact.

I received a three-page thank-you letter from Sally. I shared it with the others. Its words resonated deeply with us, particularly a line that stood out:

"Chaplain Jim, Aaron, and Clarence, I never knew people like you really existed. Thank you for your care of our family." It was a poignant reminder of the impact we can have, often in ways we never fully realize.

I remember that, while on the scene, I wanted and prayed that I could let Ray know that his daughter's life mattered. In the end, I couldn't. However, God could.

Here is the letter I received from Clarence.

> Jim,
>
> I'm grateful for the chance to discuss how we supported Taylor's family and how our actions profoundly affected both the teachers and students.
>
> I clearly remember speaking with some of her former teachers; we all wanted to do something. However, our office manager provided helpful information on navigating the restrictions. She offered more insight into the district's involvement and the decisions we made. Her teachers agreed that doing nothing wasn't an option. The school district superintendent explained that they had planted trees for memorials, but now no one remembers who they were honoring. The result is the district has decided against continuing to allow memorials.
>
> The district ultimately decided against creating any permanent memorials. Our pending move to a new building partly influenced this decision; they wanted to avoid them there. Additionally, our guidance and counseling departments were concerned that permanent memorials might perpetuate student sadness.
>
> I understood the rationale behind not opting for something permanent. For instance, the old school had a giant mural dedicated to a sixth-grade teacher. It was large and dominated the library. However, it had been there for so long, even before my time, that its original significance had faded. No one remembered the teacher it honored.
>
> So, after repeated requests, the district reluctantly agreed to allow a temporary memorial instead, allowing us to put something up briefly. I went beyond that, creating a poster in memory of her and keeping it up for the rest of the school year, not just a month or two. Our office assistant, now retired, also kept a small photo of Taylor as part of her office decor. She kept it displayed for a couple of years. It was a subtle tribute but meaningful to the teachers.
>
> We found ways to honor her memory quietly. Our principal was understanding, allowing us to keep the smaller, subtle memorials. There's something I haven't mentioned yet. After you and I visited the grandmother, she sent a heartfelt card to the school.

Along with it were individually laminated feathers inscribed with "Thank You." It was a touching gesture from her, these tokens of appreciation. I handed them out to Taylor's teachers, each receiving a feather as a special thank you from the grandmother. She wanted to express gratitude for their impact on her granddaughter's life. I had saved one of these feathers for you, intending to give it to you as well, but I can't find it.

As the school year drew to a close, we faced a decision about including her in our yearbook, specifically whether to add her picture or not. We unanimously felt it was important to remember her in this way. I remember a girl who was Taylor's close friend. They had shared many experiences together. I thought it would also be significant for her to see Taylor included in the class photos.

Besides including her picture, we decided to add a photo of the poster I had created. It was a small tribute but meaningful for the students. It marked a poignant moment for them.

Eventually, both grandmothers learned about our tribute in the yearbook and requested copies. I had already met the one grandmother with you, but then I had the chance to meet the other grandmother at school. She was deeply moved when she visited. We had a heartfelt conversation, and she was so grateful that Taylor's memory was being honored in this way. It was striking to see both grandmothers together that day, united in their appreciation of our efforts to keep Taylor's story alive.

I recall when you mentioned the idea of creating a memorial for her at school, provided it was permitted. I remember how she looked into your eyes silently for a long minute. It seemed she was searching for sincerity in your gaze, trying to discern if your proposal was genuine.

Jim, this all happened because you suggested that we reach out to Taylor's maternal grandmother.

God Bless,
Clarence

Insights

There are unique emotional complexities involved with the death of a child:

- Acknowledge the uniqueness of their grief: Each grief journey is deeply personal and unique, especially when it involves the loss of a young child. It's important to acknowledge this uniqueness and allow the family to experience their emotions without judgment or expectation. There is no "right way" to grieve such a profound loss.

- Create space for memories: Encourage the family to share stories and memories of their daughter. This can be a powerful way to honor her life and can provide comfort amidst the pain. Creating a memory book, planting a garden, or other physical memorials can serve as enduring reminders of her impact on their lives.

- Recognize the grief of siblings: If there are siblings, recognize that their grief might manifest differently. Young siblings may not fully understand the concept of death and may need additional support through counseling or therapy. Older siblings might take on roles of strength to support their parents, sometimes at the expense of their own grieving process.

- Encourage professional support: Advocate for professional grief counseling or support groups. These resources can offer structured guidance and provide a community that understands the path of bereavement. Professional support can be crucial in helping the family navigate their grief healthily and constructively.

- My time as a chaplain has shown me the importance of involving multiple chaplains in complex situations. It goes beyond simply dividing up tasks; it's about forming more profound, more meaningful connections with those who are grieving. This method enables us to give personalized support by focusing on different family members, helping to build trust and understanding. While Aaron dedicated his attention to one group, I could concentrate on another, giving everyone involved the best chance to receive the required care and attention.

Reflections on the Holy Spirit

We could feel the Holy Spirit working throughout the event. Here are just a few of the ways:

- I was only a short distance from the scene.
- Two chaplains were available to help with the complex family dynamics.
- Aaron and I quickly received the family's trust and the grandmothers' cooperation from the start.

- The medical examiner was willing to wait for the mother to arrive for almost an hour longer than normal. She even delayed responding to another scene.
- Clarence was part of our small group and also one of Taylor's favorite teachers.
- Clarence had a desire to provide support at his school, which reached out to bless Taylor's family.

CHAPTER 10

Under the Shadow of Wings and a Flag: A Testament of Hope

> The World War II generation shares so many common values: duty, honor, country, personal responsibility, and the marriage vow "For better or for worse"—it was the last generation in which, broadly speaking, marriage was a commitment and divorce was not an option.
>
> —Tom Brokaw

EARLY IN THE MORNING, with the world outside still half asleep, I was rummaging through my car for my responder coat when I discovered the flag I had purchased weeks ago was still in a bag. I'd forgotten it was there. I bought it to replace the tattered one on my flag pole. To me, it was never just a piece of fabric. It is a reminder of all the hopes, struggles, and sacrifices wrapped up in those stars and stripes. Today, I discovered the reason this flag remained in my car.

My pager read:

- M 84
- UA
- Address

In the silence that followed the last echoes of victory, amidst the joy and tears marking the end of the Second World War, most stories remained untold, sacrifices unseen. Amidst the small, nearly forgotten moments, the courage of a generation whispered the loudest. Entering the resident's private room in an adult group home, I saw an old photo of a man in uniform leaning on a tank. His dirty uniform, without medals, still conveyed a tale of courage. It was more than a faded photograph to me; it was a portal to the past, inviting us to listen, remember, and honor the silent vows of a generation that shaped our lives today. Though fading with the passing of time, their voices still carry the timeless message of resilience, sacrifice, and the unbreakable human spirit.

The police requested I meet with the family at a small assisted-care group home. John's wife of almost fifty years died eleven years before, and he had lived by himself until four years ago. That was when he fell and broke his hip. After some problems with him remembering to take his medications, he and his son had to decide what to do next, knowing that whatever they decided would affect John for the rest of his life. He needed a caregiver living at his home. However, because of the high cost, it was not a viable solution. The other option was for John to move into an assisted-care facility. We expected his son, daughter-in-law, and their children to arrive within the next few hours.

My observation was that, as with many residents of care facilities, they had expected his death for some time. However, even when someone's death is imminent, family and friends still experience surprise at the intensity of grief they feel. It is common for people to leave unspoken words and leave thank yous and apologies unresolved.

When I arrived, John's body was visible in the community room, fifteen feet from the front door. He lay covered with a sheet behind an oversized couch. Six other residents were in the room and a staff member whose eyes told me she had been crying, and the TV was on. However, they did not seem to pay any attention to the program and whispered to each other.

Seeing someone on the staff affected by death was something I would pass on to the families, and it usually had a strong positive effect. Another thing I often find familiar with the family is the guilt of the sons and daughters. They would want to explain why they had not visited their parents. Even though they had excellent reasons, they still experienced guilt. Learning the staff had formed a strong bond with their parents often helped.

Awkward is an excellent description of how I felt my presence was being received in the room. Initially, they took the residents to their rooms until the medics stopped trying to revive John. Then, the director/owner gave the residents the option to remain in their rooms until the funeral home personnel had removed his body, or if they wanted, they could return to the dayroom, which they did. In those few hours with them, I came to sense that their relationship with each other was very much like a family. They had created a safe place to say whatever was on their mind. While talking to the manager, I overheard someone say they would miss John, and another person added, "Also, his wit." I excused myself from the manager and went to talk with the residents in the main room.

I asked if I could have the privilege of talking with them for a few minutes. The woman in the overstuffed chair returned immediately with "About what?" "I overheard someone say that John had a quick wit. Sharing that impression with his son would mean a lot to him. It would tell the family he found a place where he fit in. It might also help with the guilt that families often experience following the decision to place a parent in a care facility." No one said anything for a while, and then Frank, the man in the wheelchair, offered, "Please join us." Two men sat on the couch, which blocked John's body from view, and residents or staff occupied most of the other chairs. Picking up a chair from the dining room, I joined them.

At first, the conversations stopped with me there, but then the man in the wheelchair asked who I was. I explained that I served as a chaplain with fire and police. Then the same man asked, "Why would the police have you come here?" "Good question. I am here for John's family. They wanted me to be available in case John's son needed help to make any arrangements or could use some available resources and to be available in case anyone had questions." That answer relaxed them, but I still felt like an outsider. They were protective of their group, which I thought was good.

It took answering a few more questions before they decided I was safe to talk with. Then, I wondered if there was anything they might share with me when I spoke with John's son. That opened the door to some stories about John while he was living here in this home and some stories he had told them that his son knew nothing about.

While waiting for John's son to arrive, I asked to see John's room, hoping it might offer some insight before speaking with the family. I noticed military decorations and a photograph of him in an army uniform. Another photo showed a platoon of soldiers standing before a tank, confirming that he had served in World War II.

When the family arrived, they explained he had been in this home for over three years. Most families felt terrible about how seldom they visited their relatives. The son was mentally in the same place as he started our conversation with his regrets for missed visiting opportunities. He had wanted to move him closer to them, but his dad had resisted. He liked it here, and he hoped to finish here.

The son received a promotion a few years ago, but that required him to move closer to his job. Then, because of their kid's school activities, sports, and their involvement in a new church, they were experiencing guilt for not making visiting his dad more of a priority. He explained they had visited regularly at first, but then their other commitments got in the way. Families often repeat that comment with someone in long-term care. Knowing he liked it here and had developed close friendships with the others made their decision to let him remain at this group home easier to accept. Attempting to move him closer to them would have been for their convenience, not his.

When the funeral home attendants arrived, they filled out the required forms with the information provided by the family and then left to get their gurney and body bag. I followed them to their van. It amazes me when I can trace the Lord's intervention and timing. I enjoy the surprises when they occur. This time, I purchased a large flag for my home flagpole weeks before. The flag was still in my car. It was about the same size as the military flag used to cover caskets.

Giving it to the funeral home crew, I asked them if they would use it to cover John's gurney before lifting it into view. The family had moved into the kitchen at my request. I did not want them to witness John being put into a body bag.

I also wanted to honor this man who had served our country. The funeral home attendants exceeded my expectations with their exceptional service. They stood at attention with a dignified poise, briskly snapping the flag taut between them before respectfully lowering it out of sight. That got everyone's interest. They kept the gurney positioned behind the couch, ensuring it remained out of sight and too low for John's family and others in the room to see anything. But as they slowly raised the gurney, the solemn scene became visible to everyone: John draped gracefully with the flag, a symbol of honor and respect.

My peripheral vision drew my attention to the man in the wheelchair. He began by reaching down and flipping up the footrests that supported his legs. Then, he placed his feet on the floor using his hands and began sliding forward in the seat. His arms trembled as he rose out of the chair. Two nurses ran to stop him, but he stubbornly asked them to let him do this. Finally, once he stood, though still unsteady, he came to attention. Although trembling, he turned slightly and slowly saluted John's earth suit. He stood at attention, his tears visible as they rolled John out, the flag draped over him. My attention was initially solely on Frank as he struggled to stand. But then, something remarkable happened. As I watched him, I saw everyone in the room had also risen to their feet, joining Frank in a unified salute. This spontaneous gesture of respect and solidarity was profoundly moving. Later, during a follow-up call, I spoke with John's family. They shared with me how much this moment meant to them and how it blessed them to see such a powerful display of honor and support for their father. It was a testament to John's impact on everyone in that room. Some things leave a profound impression. For me, the determination on that man's face as he struggled to rise to his feet out of respect for his friend is a memory I still cherish.

American goldfinch, the state bird of Washington

During my time with John's family, a bird flew into the room through the front door. It was flying around, crashing into the windows and landing on the open rafters of the dayroom. The staff said it had happened several times before, and they had had a terrible time catching it before they injured themselves. This bird was an American goldfinch, the state bird of Washington. The nurses tried to capture it each time, but it would take off whenever they got close.

It continued to fly around the room and against the closed windows, missing the open ones. I watched the staff try to catch it for a few minutes, then offered to help. They dared me, "If you think you can catch it, please do." With that open challenge, I walked over to the window, where the bird was now perched on a rafter over my head. I tried to reach up and grab it slowly. But it retook flight, flew around the room, and crashed again into a window. However, this time, it landed near my feet and appeared stunned. Reaching down, I quickly picked it up. Once in my hands, its racing heart slowed down as I walked to the door. I intended to open the sliding door and let it go. But when I extended my arms and removed my top hand, the bird remained and only tilted its head back and forth as it looked at me.

It remained perched on my hand, and the room behind me became quiet. The bright yellow bird stood there, staring back at me. I drifted my hand back and forth, expecting the bird to leave. However, it just stood there. Then, hopping, it grabbed my index finger like a pet parakeet might. That astounded me, and I stopped shaking my hand.

After pausing for a few moments, the goldfinch shifted again, this time coming to rest facing the room. I waved my hand more vigorously in response, yet the bird clung on with surprising tenacity. The wild bird's reaction was unexpected, almost as if it sensed my intentions were good. When I held my hand steady, the bird, in a moment of trust, hopped gently and settled on my ring finger. This encounter, filled with tentative movements and mutual curiosity, spanned over a minute. Eventually, the goldfinch soared away as I shook my hand with greater force. I turned to close the door and noticed everyone's eyes were on me, their faces a mix of wonder and intrigue.

I considered that the people here might be mainly waiting for their time to run out. Their families would visit occasionally, but they primarily existed isolated in this environment. What could the bird have experienced that caused it to feel safe in my grip? I began thinking out loud, wondering why it took so long to leave. How could the bird have known that it was secure in my hands?

Everyone had watched the bird's reaction as it rested on my hand and saw me try to shake it off. I again pondered aloud if we all might have something in common with this bird—that got everyone's attention—then elaborated that we are all fearful of what comes next as we age. We know so little of what happens after death. I asked them, "Shouldn't the goldfinch typically be terrified of being held by a human and fly away the moment my hand opened? Yet, in this instance, it seemed to understand that it wasn't in danger, sensing no need to escape immediately."

"Think about this goldfinch," I continued. "Why didn't it rush to escape when it could? Maybe it could be similar to us in this way, feeling unsure about stepping into the unknown. However, once there, what if the fear no longer existed? We all hold tight to this life, our familiar ground, because what comes next, in heaven, is a mystery."

I went on, looking around at the nodding heads, "But just imagine, once we're there, maybe we'll find a peace we never knew and wonder why we ever felt afraid. This goldfinch, in its small way, trusted me. It was terrifying for the bird, like anyone entering an unfamiliar place. But immediately, it found comfort, even in the unknown." I took a moment, allowing the weight of my words to settle in the air. "This tiny creature, in the safety of my hand, embraced an unfamiliar experience, a venture into an unknown world. Perhaps it's a reminder to us all that beyond our current knowledge and experiences, there lies beauty and tranquility waiting to be discovered."

Afterward, the group home's owner graciously offered coffee to John's family and me. Seated around the dining table, I inquired about the inspiration behind his work with older adults. He then shared a heartfelt personal experience from years ago when he faced finding suitable care for his father.

He explained that, based on recommendations, he had placed his dad in a larger facility specifically designed for residents with memory loss. However, during his visits, he couldn't help but notice how the staff interacted with the other residents. They would lead the residents into a spacious room adorned with paintings—some abstract, others depicting flowers—and a big-screen TV.

What troubled him was the lack of engagement from the attendants. After situating the residents in front of the paintings or chairs, they often left them unattended, seemingly more interested in their conversations. This neglect persisted, even when he spent a few hours visiting his father.

He noticed that the TV, typically left on a cooking channel, had no relevance to the male residents seated before it.

The owner's deep emotional connection to his father's care profoundly affected him, sparking a solid motivation to create a superior environment for older adults needing compassionate care. This pivotal experience ultimately led him to establish his own group home, where genuine attention and empathy would be the guiding principles.

He felt those residents had lost their dignity. Since he had done well working for Microsoft and no longer needed to work, he retired and created this home not just to help the guests but also so the guests could interact with others. He described the type of people he sought to help support his guests.

Some additional residents joined John's family at the table. As they shared stories of John's wit and remarkable ability to recall historical facts, laughter filled the room. It seemed like every memory brought a fresh burst of laughter, underscoring the depth of affection everyone held for him.

As the conversation continued, the group affirmed the owner's vision and goals for the place. Their enthusiasm resonated, and this group home was more than just a building; it was a place that celebrated each individual, honoring their uniqueness and creating a genuine sense of belonging.

The heartfelt exchange of stories brought comfort and reassurance to John's family, affirming their decision to leave him in this caring community. When they departed, they knew that John had been part of a supportive community and that he had made a meaningful difference there.

I've always cherished the opportunity to engage with older generations. The act of asking questions and listening to their perspectives is incredibly insightful. They often express their views with refreshing honesty, unbound by the constraints of political correctness, leading me to ask if they would tell me about the experiences that had significantly shaped their lives.

The first to speak was Clair. She was ninety-eight years old. She said the thing she enjoyed most growing up was when her family first got running hot water and described how they lived before it became available.

During our conversation, Frank and I delved into memories, and he shared stories about a 1932 Ford three-window coup that he and his buddies had hot-rodded after the war. When he mentioned serving in Patton's Third Army, I informed him that my uncle, whom I was named after, had also served in Patton's Third Army but was killed in France. Frank looked at me for a moment and nodded in acknowledgment.

Intrigued, I asked Frank if he had ever shared his wartime experiences with his family. His quick response was heartfelt, "Never! Retelling the events causes me to relive them. There is no way for me to use words to describe my emotions, fear, guilt, and scars from that time."

Given the topic's sensitivity, I asked Frank for advice, sharing that occasionally, I encounter children of war veterans wondering why their fathers never spoke about their wartime experiences.

He offered me some advice: "Please tell them that those times of struggling to do what was required by their fathers and loved ones to survive was not something they could recall without guilt and regret. Most war veterans involved in action live with the memories of things they never want to revisit."

In this way, Frank's wisdom sheds light on the profound impact war experiences can have on veterans, urging us to approach such subjects with empathy and understanding.

"Betty, do you have any thoughts or advice when I meet with families?" She started with "Why do people complain so much now? Setbacks are just part of life, even if it is a life-changing event. During our time as missionaries in Africa, my husband and I operated an orphanage for children who had lost their parents to death or violence. The orphans had almost nothing, but somehow, they were happier than our kids here, who get almost everything they ask for. Search on YouTube for African orphanages, and you will witness the kids' joy and their support for one another. Unfortunately, our kids have learned to use smartphones to communicate but no longer know how to have meaningful conversations or develop close friendships. The true cost of texting and messaging to relationships is unknown. However, I believe it may affect their ability to enjoy relationships as strong as we have had."

I ask for the privilege of praying for them before leaving. Frank delighted me when he also prayed.

As I walked toward the door, Frank rolled up to me. He said he wanted to speak to me for a second. He said, "I became a pastor after serving as a soldier during World War II until retiring about fifteen years ago. Watching you with that bird was an unbelievable experience. What you said was perfect for what we need to hear as we wait for our time to run out. Thank you for being bold."

Insights

- I always enjoyed it when I had the chance to spend time with those from a previous generation. The conversations were often fascinating and helpful for my ministry. I found they had tremendous wisdom and insight to share when asking for advice or their opinions. Their awareness and knowledge came from first-hand experiences, not only from something they read or saw on TV.
- It was also common for many from the earlier generations to enjoy decades of strong marriages. As a result, one of my favorite questions was, "What do you think was the secret to keeping your marriage so strong?" I learned to appreciate when they would become the teacher—sharing what life taught them. It was a gift to me. Of course, this often led to other topics, and I saw them become more animated as they spoke.
- Another conversation starter I often used was simply asking for advice. It could be random, about anything. When someone would share an interest or hobby they had, it was a privilege that led to more questions. It was almost like turning a switch on for them. Those of the previous generations have so much knowledge learned through their experiences but no one to share it with. Many grandparents share the experience of feeling sidelined, their rich reservoir of knowledge and skills often going unrecognized by younger generations, including their grandkids. In today's fast-paced world, younger generations might not fully appreciate the deep joy and invaluable insights that come from engaging in conversations with older people. Older individuals offer a treasure trove of experiences, wisdom, and stories that bridge the gap between past and present and provide unique perspectives that enrich understanding and empathy. The delight in these interactions goes beyond mere conversation; it's about connecting with living history, learning lessons no textbook can teach, and recognizing the value of diverse experiences. These dialogues were not just exchanges of words, but offered opportunities for meaningful connections.

Reflections on the Holy Spirit's Help During This Call

The goldfinch was not just any bird, as I discovered while writing this chapter.

Many calls made a lasting impression on me, not just because they provided undeniable help from the Holy Spirit, but also because of the delivery method. This time, it was a bird to open a conversation about heaven, one that allowed me to share hope and comfort.

Out of curiosity, I googled "birds in the Bible." What showed up along with the results was how we used different birds as symbols to represent an emotion or quality of life and other things.

When the google search results came up, this was at the very bottom of the first page: What bird represents the soul? That piqued my interest. Clicking on it revealed,

> What does a Goldfinch symbolize in the Bible?
> A very general reading of the Goldfinch might, therefore, remind the viewer that his soul is "in the hands" of God. The bird could also be seen as a symbol of the Resurrection of Christ.
>
> A Goldfinch is a small bird sometimes depicted in paintings of the Christ Child; it is usually shown being held in his hands but is sometimes attached to a string.[1]

Of all the birds in the world, a goldfinch perched on my hand that day—symbolic, for someone's soul is in the hands of God. It closely aligns with what I said that day.

The flag had lain forgotten in my car, still in a shopping bag resting beneath some fishing supplies and my responder coat, a casualty of life's relentless pace, waiting for the right time to unveil itself. It wasn't until I reached for my coat on the call that I discovered it again. That day, it was transformed from an overlooked item into a profound symbol of unity and strength. Since then, the flag has always remained in my car, always available.

---

1. See also Johnson, Philip. "Goldfinch: Symbol of the Resurrection." Animals Matter to God, June 3, 2012. https://animalsmattertogod.com/2012/06/03/goldfinch-symbol-for-resurrection/.

CHAPTER 11

Praise You in This Storm

I will give thanks to the Lord because of his righteousness; I will sing the praises of the name of the Lord Most High.

—Ps 7:17 NIV

It was a blessing to be there that day. Most of my calls were to assist the families with making final arrangements and do whatever I could to help the grieving family members. I would listen, offer prayer, help with calls, provide guidance or suggestions, and be there for anyone to talk to if they had needs. This one was different.

My pager read:

- M 44
- CPR
- Address

Experiencing the loss of someone dear can be a profound spiritual challenge. While navigating this arduous journey, it helps to consider that grief, although painful, can ultimately lead to a deeper appreciation for life and a more substantial reliance on the promises of Christ. The part a chaplain plays is in our ability to offer unwavering support, patience, and kindness to grieving families as they cope with these profound losses.

Flanked by their sergeant, two sheriff's deputies met me at the apartment door with a stoic presence. They wordlessly invited me to step inside. I needed a moment to process the scene that greeted me: Talia sprawled on the living room floor and a shattered bathroom door leaning eerily against a wall.

My memories of that day are still vivid, recalling the weight of sorrow in the room. Learning the mother had tragically lost another son a little less than a year prior was part of it. During the chaos of activity, I closed my eyes and whispered a silent prayer, hoping to find the words to comfort this grieving family. I also prayed for an opportunity to share the strength and comfort my faith provided. However, that was not to be. It was this family that blessed me.

As responders bustled around, a cousin of the deceased approached, offering a glimpse into the events that had unfolded earlier. The deceased's twelve-year-old niece, a budding basketball star at her school, had playfully challenged Talia to a one-on-one game. They'd spent an hour on the court, laughing and competing. With cheeks flushed from exertion, they made their way indoors. The mother was preparing a family dinner, so he excused himself to shower. They all heard the loud bang from the bathroom. They called 911 when they found the door blocked, and Talia would not respond or open it.

The conversation between firefighters and sheriff's deputies interrupted the story. Their movements were methodical in search of their medical pack, which carried all essentials, meds, and opioids for trauma care.

I approached the mother, unsure if her son had been married, and gently inquired if she was the next of kin. I was also trying to understand more about the relationship of all those in the room. Through tear-filled eyes, she shared her son was visiting from Florida. He intended to spend a week with her before they would journey together to a large family reunion in Samoa.

Talia lay there, now covered with a white sheet. He was the elder of her two sons. The memory of his younger brother, Arihi, who had died the previous year, cast a shadow in the room. Seeing the photos of the younger brother placed around the room told me the family was still dealing with the ever-present reminder of their shared grief from his loss. It also reminded me that every day was a gift and not to take it for granted that I would be here tomorrow.

Every corner of the room testified to their deep-seated faith. Intricate Christian ornaments, each carrying a unique narrative, beautified the bookshelves. Meanwhile, a well-thumbed Bible, its pages bearing the gentle wear of many contemplative hours, occupied a revered spot on the coffee table.

I felt safe asking if I could offer a prayer for her son. "Yes, please," she responded, her voice quivering. She took hold of my sleeve, almost dragging me closer to him. As I settled on the hardwood floor, my head bowed and my hand resting lightly on the sheet that draped his body, a subtle shift occurred in the room as the family joined us to pray. Often, there is a reluctance to touch someone's body, but not here. The family and friends surprised me when they reached out without hesitation and put a hand on the sheet covering Talia's body as I began praying.

The deputies and firefighters, who had continued searching, froze in place. They were supportive with how they treated the families and seemed to know what I needed.

I sent a silent prayer, hoping my words would comfort the grieving families and trusting that God would guide my speech. My prayer had a noticeable effect on the family, and it was encouraging to see that it was because of the clarity and precision of my words. By the time I finished, emotions had swelled, apparent in the tears that glistened in nearly every eye present.

I learned from his mother what Talia's name meant. I needed to look it up later because I couldn't read my notes. This is the meaning of the name Talia (this was the first time I heard that name): "Talia comes from the Samoan word 'fa'atali' and means 'to wait.' The word is often used as a reference to waiting or being in anticipation for something big, which is 'Second Coming of the Lord.' This name will remind your child to be deeply rooted in the Christian faith."[1]

As I mingled with the relatives and friends gathered in the room, their stories vividly depicted Talia. I learned about his magnetic personality, hobbies, and undeniable passion for life. Among these tales, I uncovered the story of today's events. Just forty-five minutes before the tragedy, Talia had been playing basketball with his niece, enjoying the exercise and laughter.

---

1. Ahmed, Arshi. "75 Pretty Pacific Islander Baby Names for Boys and Girls." MomJunction, last updated on Oct. 14, 2024. Para. 6. https://www.momjunction.com/articles/pacific-islander-baby-names_00400744/#:~:text=Talia,Second%20Coming%20of%20the%20Lord.

Once their game had concluded, Talia headed to the bathroom to shower. Shortly after that, an alarming bang echoed through the apartment. Concern turned to panic when Talia didn't respond from behind the bathroom door. The family's frantic calls to 911 brought the fire department and EMTs rushing to the scene. The responders broke into the bathroom with force and discovered Talia was unresponsive. They moved him to the adjoining living room to administer CPR. Despite their efforts, they couldn't revive him.

To introduce a measure of peace amidst the turmoil, I asked for a pillow and gently placed it under Talia's head. This simple gesture comforts grieving families by showing respect.

As I spoke with Talia's mother, the earlier basketball game came up again, highlighting the niece's role in coaxing Talia into playing. This detail now took on a new significance in my mind. My attention shifted to the niece, who had retreated to a quiet corner of the apartment. Isolated from the others, she seemed lost in her thoughts, perhaps wrestling with guilt. I assumed the question lingering in her mind might be that she blamed herself for what happened—thinking her playful challenge to play basketball had somehow led to her uncle's death.

I wanted to make sure she knew it wasn't her fault he had died. It became vital for her to grasp this before she started blaming herself. She might have thought I was trying to make her feel better if I had told her it was not your fault. So, as I sat beside her on the floor, searching for the right words, an idea suddenly came to me. When I shared it with her, she looked up and smiled, showing she understood.

As I approached a deputy, a touching sight stopped me. The niece had picked up Talia's guitar, the one he had used to lead worship at his church in Florida. She was cradling it as one would a cherished infant. After a while, the faintest sound of strings being gently picked reached my ears. When I glanced back at her, I saw a distant look, a kind of wistful reflection, as if she were drifting back to a cherished moment in time and a bittersweet memory.

Drawn to her, I approached her again and asked if she remembered any of her uncle's favorite songs. She acknowledged with a nod, her eyes meeting mine. "Do you think Talia might appreciate hearing one of them?" I gently proposed. I didn't expect her to move from her spot, but she surprised me. With a determined grace, she moved, positioning herself beside

Talia on the floor. Her voice wove a melody as her fingers played the strings again.

One of my favorite sayings is, "If you really want to get their attention, whisper."

No one else in the room could understand the words the niece was singing; however, the conversations stopped. Then, slowly, her playing changed. The guitar became louder, and the sound of her words grew until we could not miss what she was singing. Unlike most kids her age, who are shy, she possessed a beautiful voice that seemed to bloom with confidence as she sang. With her eyes gently closed, shutting out all distractions, she poured her heart into the song, singing solely for her uncle.

We were all still sitting on the floor when she sang loud enough so we could recognize what she was singing. My memory of her sitting beside her uncle, playing his guitar and singing, still lingers.

"It Is Well with My Soul" was the song.

Surrounding Talia on the floor, the family and friends subtly harmonized with the niece's song while gently reaching their hands to rest on the sheet, enveloping Talia. The scene and sound immediately stopped the first responders. They stood still, briefly looked at me, and then their eyes fixed in wonder at those gathered on the floor. At the beginning of the second verse, the niece's voice surged with emotion, and the voices around her rose in unison. This scene also remains locked in my memory: the grieving mother, surrounded by family, tears streaming down their face, lifting praise songs over the body of her son who had died mere moments before.

Surprisingly, the container the responders had been searching for had been hiding in plain sight the entire time, and they finally located it. The reason it eluded them earlier became apparent to me: they were still supposed to be here.

Just as they were preparing to leave, the niece's song caught their attention. They stopped in their tracks, captivated. The deputy standing at the door disappeared, only to reappear a moment later, now accompanied by the other deputy and the sergeant. Together, they stood in awe at the doorway as the room resonated with praise songs over Talia's body.

The firefighters should have been gone twenty-five minutes earlier. They had to remain until they found their missing supply of medications. The sergeant and the deputies had also stayed beyond their time for the same reason. Now, it was as if the overt presence of the opioid container faded against the sheer weight of the moment.

When the Spirit says move, you have to move. I never expected to hear the sheriff's deputies and firefighters join in as we sang "Amazing Grace." But it happened. First, the sergeant joined in, then the others. After that song, the crew from Station 10 left, and all but one deputy. He would remain until the medical examiner arrived.

Later, I thanked the family for allowing me to be there with them at this difficult time and asked if I could read the Twenty-Third Psalm (KJV) before I left. The mother said she would like that. I stood to reach into my wallet where I kept a laminated copy. As I did that, the rest of the room stood up. I told them they didn't have to stand, but they corrected me by explaining that they always stood out of respect when reading Scripture.

I started, then stopped when they all joined in. Politely asking if they would only listen this time, I started again.

The Lord is my shepherd—*That's relationship*
I shall not want—*That's supply*
He maketh me to lie down in green pastures—*That's rest*
He leadeth me beside the still waters—*That's refreshment*
He restoreth my soul—*That's healing*
He leadeth me in the paths of righteousness—*That's guidance*
For his namesake—*That's purpose*
Yea, though I walk through the valley of the shadow of death—
That's testing
I will fear no evil—*That's protection*
For thou art with me—*That's faithfulness*
Thy rod and thy staff they comfort me—*That's discipline*
Thou preparest a table before me in the presence of mine enemies—
That's hope
Thou anointest my head with oil—*That's consecration*
My cup runneth over—*That's abundance*
Surely goodness and mercy shall follow me all the days of my life—
That's blessing
And I will dwell in the house of the Lord—*That's security*
Forever—*That's eternity*

All said amen at the same time.

Insights

- There was always a difference when I answered a call with Christians. There was still a sense of loss and emotional pain when someone died. However, the expectation of meeting again in heaven changed their outlook. Plus, they had joy and reassurance that their loved one was experiencing no more pain and an incredible reunion.
- Back at Station 10, the firefighters talked about what they had seen. Over the following months, it opened some opportunities with the firefighters.

Reflections on the Holy Spirit

Speaking with the niece when she had retreated to the chair away from the others, I wanted her to understand she wasn't at fault for Talia's death. However, she needed to come to see this truth on her own. Just telling her might have felt like I was only trying to comfort her, not sharing the truth. The idea came to me so quickly, and I can't take credit for it. I used an example from recently fixing the fan belt in my car. Since I was the last one to drive before it broke, I wondered if that meant I had caused the failure, or if it was simply the result of use. When she looked directly at me and smiled, I could tell she understood what I was asking, and at that moment, I felt a sense of connection between us.

CHAPTER 12

Where the Blacktop Ends

"Leprosy." The Jewish law, Lev 13:1, prohibited anyone with such a disease from associating with the general community. They had to be isolated and, many times, lived as outcasts until they died. It makes me wonder whether they would have cast drug addicts aside, isolating them in the same way we often do today.

A profound sense of isolation was present as I arrived at the scene. The halfway house on a dirt road extending beyond the end of a paved street was a stark contrast to the upscale neighborhood I had just traversed. This stark contrast likely amplified the residents' feelings of detachment from the more affluent parts of society.

My pager read:

- F 24
- OD
- Address

The transition from the neighboring area to this location was surreal. After passing homes that exuded a sense of pride on their quarter-acre lots, I found myself in front of a sprawling property that spanned one and a half acres. The house, visibly in need of attention, starkly contrasted with its surroundings. Dense foliage and towering evergreen cedar trees flanked the lane, serving as a natural barrier and effectively shielding the house from the prying eyes of the nearby residents.

Upon arrival, I encountered a cluster of emergency vehicles and limited parking options. I had to decide between parking under a tree full of birds and risking them being over my car. The other option was parking in the driveway of the last house on the right. Opting for the latter, I couldn't help but ponder how the presence of a halfway house might have affected the neighboring homeowners, a thought that filled me with empathy.

After parking in the neighbor's driveway, I approached the door to seek permission for my car. Through the blinds, I could see the homeowner watching me approach. He opened the door, and I introduced myself, asking if leaving my car in his driveway was acceptable. He agreed. Gesturing toward the dirt lane, he inquired about the activity around "those people." I summarized the suspected overdose case. His resigned response, "That's to be expected, I guess," echoed a weary acceptance. Seizing the moment, I offered to return later with an update. To my relief, he seemed interested. I realized it could be an excellent opportunity to provide further insights, a gesture that I hoped would convey my empathy and concern for the community.

The neighborhood was on edge about the new halfway house. Concerns over safety, disruptions, and falling property values fueled widespread unease. The community rallied together, protesting to block the county's plans at every legal turn. Despite their fervent efforts, the county prevailed.

The incident occurred in an unincorporated area, leaving the sheriff's department and Fire District 1's medics in charge. The medical examiners were over an hour away. Until their arrival, the scene—where the body lay face up on the back deck amidst drug paraphernalia like needles, a bent spoon, and rubber tubing—remained untouched.

As the fentanyl crisis worsened, a disturbing numbness had taken hold among the first responders. Empathy for overdose victims, once keen, now seemed dulled by resigned acceptance of the grim reality. Yet, the call I attended stood out. Deputies glanced at me with puzzled expressions, questioning the need for spiritual support in a tragedy deemed self-inflicted. "After all, she knew the risks," they seemed to concur.

Somehow, this call stood out as an exception to the unsettling trend. Upon my arrival, law enforcement officers, seasoned by countless emergencies, painted a familiar yet distinct description. Their puzzled looks in my direction spoke volumes, mirroring the collective uncertainty about the necessity of my role in this scenario. An unspoken question was obvious: What difference could a chaplain make in facing such a grim reality? The fire department's chief requested a chaplain, but the sheriff apologized for interfering with my plans for the day.

A young girl lost too soon to the sickness of addiction lay silent, her story never to be finished, but her struggles were over. The delay in her family's arrival left a void for me. Usually, I speak with the family first. The house, a sanctuary for those wrestling with their demons of substance use, now found itself at the heart of a sad reflection on the fragile journey of recovery. Even the director, himself a testament to the possibility of success, seemed to embody the complexity of hope and despair that characterizes the battle against addiction.

At this moment, my presence might have appeared superfluous to most, an additional figure in a scene already too crowded with grief, blame, and unanswered questions. Yet, this perspective overlooked the essence of my calling. Beyond the immediate tragedy, my role was to bridge the gap between earthly despair and heavenly hope. It was an opportunity to reaffirm the value of every life, to counteract the creeping numbness with a reminder of our shared humanity.

As I navigated the delicate dynamics of this call, I was acutely aware of the undercurrents of judgment and misunderstanding that can accompany such losses. The challenge was to provide comfort and gently remind all present of the depth of compassion at the heart of our Savior. In doing so, I hoped to give a glimpse of understanding and empathy in this hardened routine tragedy, offering a space where healing could begin.

Like many others, this call underscored the profound complexity of my mission in the opioid crisis. Each interaction, each moment of silence, carried the weight of countless untold stories of struggle and redemption. Through these experiences, I sought to offer support and bear witness to the resilience of the human spirit in the face of overwhelming odds.

Sergeant Jeff introduced me to Mitch, the halfway house director, who quickly set the stage for my interactions with the residents. He outlined their cautious state of mind, warning me not to expect immediate openness about their struggles with addiction or family histories. His words reminded me of their defenses built around their personal stories. This briefing shaped my approach, preparing me for the reserved encounters ahead. I took Mitch's advice as both a caution and a guide, understanding that building trust with the residents would require time, empathy, and an unwavering, non-judgmental stance.

This conversation with Mitch accomplished more than just setting the scene. The expectation was to engage in surface-level exchanges and acknowledge and respect the depth of their protective silence. Understanding this dynamic was vital for my approach, emphasizing the importance of gentle outreach that honored their pace and readiness to share. Mitch's guidance proved invaluable in this environment, where every interaction carried the potential for breakthroughs or retreats. It offered a road map for engagement that balanced empathy with recognizing the residents' uniqueness in their stories.

Mitch's insights into the challenges of connecting with individuals in recovery were helpful. He spoke of the pervasive fear of judgment that haunts many battling addiction, often compounded by the belief that those without personal experience can't fully comprehend their struggles. Mitch pointed out that the perceived lack of understanding could inadvertently deepen their sense of shame. His emphasis on the subtleties of addiction, which might elude those without firsthand experience, lent a sobering perspective to the conversation. Although his words were not optimistic, what he said gave me a profound education.

Reflecting on Mitch's words, I was reminded of Sunday's sermon. My pastor, Dave, had shared the story of Jesus and the woman brought before him. Dave emphasized how Jesus not only saw her but also deeply connected with her. This inspired me to ensure that the individuals here felt truly seen and acknowledged, beyond the labels of their addiction.

Upon meeting Jill, a young woman possibly in her early twenties, I found her on the front porch, sitting with her knees drawn up and clutching a small stuffed animal. To help her feel seen and comfortable, I consciously steered clear of topics related to her addiction or past. Simple questions about her needs and interests, offering a glass of water, inquiring if she was local, or sharing her thoughts on the upcoming summer helped ease into a more natural conversation. Gradually, the topic shifted to Dakota, the young woman who had overdosed. I gently probed if she was a friend and sought her input on what positive memories or traits I could share with the family when they arrived. This question prompted her to look up at me, breaking the initial barrier and shifting the dynamic to a more open, relaxed conversation. She may have felt honored when I asked for her advice. Sometimes, in similar environments, people with an addiction are not engaged in conversation but talked down to.

As we talked about her friend, the real Dakota came into focus. She cared about her friend and wanted me to paint a picture for the family of someone friendly, often going out of her way to interact with others, and well-liked in their community. Jill spoke of the late Dakota's encouraging nature and support for those trying to overcome addiction. When I asked if I could relay her sentiments to the family, highlighting how much I valued what she shared, it seemed to affirm her worth and perspective.

The morning proved enlightening as I connected with each halfway house resident there. Each shared their unique stories and perspectives, all eager to help Dakota's family see her through their eyes. Among the insights I gathered was the intriguing choice of several residents who, preferring solitude, and had set up tents hidden among the tall evergreen trees.

After a prolonged wait, the medical examiner arrived and carefully documented the area, taking photos while consulting with Mitch to understand the timeline. Their thorough approach extended to conversations with many residents, ensuring they left with a well-rounded understanding of the situation. Shortly after completing their investigation, the sheriff's department cleared the scene.

Then, unexpectedly, Mitch approached me. The residents had planned a memorial service for Dakota that evening and specifically requested my presence. The significance of their request was clear in Mitch's expression— a mixture of surprise and profound honor.

Later, when the family arrived, we met in a private space in the dining room to discuss what would happen next while the residents discreetly stepped outside. This privacy fostered the environment needed for the sensitive conversations that were to follow.

From my experiences, I've seen how families grappling with addiction endure profound distress well before the devastating news of an overdose. Such news unleashes a storm of emotions and incredibly intense anger rooted in the grief of lost dreams for family life. Guiding these families toward forgiveness is a challenging task. By acknowledging their pain and its validity, I try to bridge the emotional gap they face. My past encounters with such deep sorrow offer a window into their fractured world.

Meeting the parents, the profound weight of their grief was unmistakable. Their eyes reflected a myriad of emotions: the breakdown of dreams, sorrow over missed chances for help, and the complex pain of loving someone who has repeatedly caused them distress. Now, with the finality of their loss, the hope for healing seemed irretrievably lost. Observing such sorrow,

I felt an innate need to offer support and comfort, not simply to be a bystander in their unspoken agony.

In addressing the complexity of addiction and its hold on both the individual and their family, I sought to redirect the anger from the person to the disease. Addiction, an overwhelming force, doesn't discriminate based on background or circumstances. Its influence goes beyond personal choices, entangled in various factors.

My goal was to ensure the family knew their loved one's life and struggles mattered. Through our conversation, I aimed to challenge the stigma surrounding deaths from drug overdose and to separate the individual's identity from their addiction. This perspective should help the family focus on positive memories, honoring the true essence of their loved one rather than the challenges cast by their addiction.

"Do you mind sharing some memories of Dakota's childhood?" I asked gently. It was a risky question. The silent answer that the father gave me was unmistakable as he folded his arms over his chest. There was a pause, and then her mother began to reminisce, slowly journeying back to when Dakota was her closest companion. Once the memories started flowing, vivid tales of family vacations filled with laughter, Dakota's infectious humor, and her love for sports came to life. A faint smile flickered across her mother's face as she recounted these happier times. Her father unexpectedly joined in, especially when sports came up, speaking with pride about Dakota's natural athletic ability. I suggested, "It would be an honor to share some of these memories with her friends at the memorial tonight if that's okay with you. Perhaps give them a glimpse of Dakota before her struggles." Their response was, "They would let me know." They called back a few hours later, saying, no, the thought that someone at the memorial might have provided the fentanyl-laced drugs to Dakota was a barrier too painful to cross. From that experience, I learned never to make such a request again.

Before I got into my car, I remembered my promise to the neighbor and rang his doorbell to provide an update. Seated at his kitchen table, I relayed the news of Dakota's passing, a name unfamiliar to him. She was just another face from the halfway house up the road to him. I tried to share the poignant moments with her grieving parents, to paint a picture of a girl who was deeply loved and missed. However, his primary concern remained any potential disturbances in the neighborhood.

Guessing at his age I inquired, "Did you serve in Vietnam?" His reply was quick: "Yes." Curious, I followed up: "Did you ever indulge in pot during your service?" His answered, "Everyone did, just to get through what we had to deal with." His eyes reflected distant memories. "Dakota started much the same way," I shared, "It seems you were one of the luckier ones." With that thought lingering, I stood up and left.

At the halfway house memorial service that evening, I found Jill sitting on the porch, waiting for me. She led me inside, candidly expressing her frustrations about living conditions in this halfway home, the meals, the movie choices, and the shared bathrooms. My amused expression caught her off guard, causing her to ask, "Why are you grinning?" "You remind me of my kids." The comparison made her laugh and put an end to her complaints.

A bonfire with logs a foot thick and three feet long greeted me when we stepped outside, radiating warmth to the circle of chairs surrounding it. It surprised me to see over forty chairs, far more than I had expected. Mingling among the attendees, I seized the opportunity to speak with several program residents who hadn't been present earlier.

As the evening air settled around us, Mitch turned to me and asked if I would open the memorial service with a prayer. Grateful for the opportunity to contribute, I nodded. Someone placed a chair in the circle where I could see everyone. I stood and offered a prayer that sought comfort and healing during their shared loss. As the last words of the prayer echoed softly in the cool night air, everyone found their seats, creating a circle of unity and reflection around the fire's glow.

The service unfolded with a solemn, intimate atmosphere reminiscent of AA meetings seen on TV, yet imbued with a deeply personal touch. Illuminated by the flickering firelight, individuals who wanted to share stood first, introducing themselves with raw honesty. Each shared their struggles with addiction before recounting their memories of Dakota. It was a tapestry of stories, weaving together diverse facets of her life. They spoke of her challenges, joys, laughter, and the brighter moments they would remember. Their words crafted a vivid portrait of Dakota, painting her as a figure of life, compassion, and humanity.

Amid these heartfelt tributes, Jill suddenly stood up. "He's the one!" she called out, pointing directly at me. Being so unexpectedly singled out in front of everyone was discomforting. Her words initially confused me, but then she added, "He talked to me like I was normal." The sincerity in her voice struck a chord with everyone present. Nods and quiet murmurs of agreement rippled through the group, each person affirming her sentiment. I realized it resulted from seeing each individual as more than their struggles.

Then, the unexpected happened. Everyone stood as if moved by an unseen script, their hands joined in a single, synchronized clap. It was a gesture of special tribute, a recognition that transcended words. Slow, unified clapping filled the night, a rhythmic testament to a shared moment of gratitude and understanding. Overwhelmed by the moment's emotion, I instinctively placed my hand over my heart, a simple yet sincere response. This gesture brought smiles and a sense of warmth to many faces in the crowd.

The service continued, but that moment of unified clapping lingered with me. It was a powerful reminder of the impact of empathy and the connections we forged through simple acts of seeing each of them, not just the addictions.

When the service ended, Jill thanked me again and hugged me. What followed was a spontaneous line of people wanting to speak with me. The experience was genuinely moving. I stayed, allowing everyone who wished to have a moment with me. The men preferred warm handshakes, while the women preferred heartfelt hugs.

As the line dwindled, those I had spoken with earlier thanked me for coming back. I prepared to leave quietly, but a few just wanted to talk. Each interaction was rich with personal stories and reflections. Being invited to this memorial service was an honor and a reminder of the difference I had experienced.

Insights

When talking to someone dealing with addiction, keep in mind the following issues:

- Fear of judgment: Those grappling with addiction often dread being judged by others unfamiliar with their struggles. There is a widespread perception that sheer willpower alone could resolve their struggles. The lack of empathy leads to feelings of shame.
- Relatability concerns: They might feel that without similar experiences, how can you understand their unique challenges?
- Reaction to unsolicited advice: People in recovery frequently hear well-meaning suggestions from those without firsthand experience.

Though often genuine, this advice is sometimes condescending or dismisses their struggles.

- Nuances of addiction: Grasping the intricate dynamics of addiction—its triggers, psychological and physical facets—can be challenging without personal experience.
- Trust and vulnerability: Openly discussing addiction requires trust. Those in recovery feel more at ease sharing their journey with someone who's walked a similar path.

Reflections on the Holy Spirit

On this call, my journey took me beyond mere observation to a profound engagement with individuals caught in the grip of drug addiction. Each story was a mosaic of choices, circumstances, and battles that many saw but few understood. As I listened and saw them not as willing participants but as victims, I felt guided by the Holy Spirit, whose gentle whispers in my heart urged me to look deeper, to see the unseen. This divine guidance did not merely change my perspective—it transformed it. It gave me a more profound empathy and a clearer understanding of the struggles faced by those in the throes of addiction. Armed with this knowledge, I was better equipped to offer not just condolences but genuine support and practical wisdom to families suffering from the unimaginable pain of losing a loved one to an overdose. In their grief, the Holy Spirit empowered me to be a beacon of hope and understanding, illuminating the path toward healing and reconciliation.

CHAPTER 13

What Was I Missing?

To acquire knowledge, one must study; but to acquire wisdom, one must observe.

—Marilyn vos Savant

As I walked away from the scene, a vital insight dawned on me—one that had eluded me amidst the chaos. I had overlooked subtle clues to the complex dynamics of the family members involved. This chapter explores moments of reflection, showing how, in the quiet aftermath, the deeper dynamics of their relationships came into focus, offering me an unexpected lesson.

The cryptic call came two hours after school let out. My pager read:

- M 16
- S
- Location

From the outset, the family dynamics struck me as delicate. Many outsiders harbor hopes of cinematic resolutions in such crises; they cling to the notion that adversity binds families tighter in love and understanding. Yet, reality can be far different. Often, when grappling with the weight of events, individuals may withdraw, overwhelmed by a torrent of emotions and thoughts. The fear of adding to the wound by uttering something inappropriate can become so paralyzing that it stifles communication. Ultimately, they find themselves entangled in either silence or physical separation, adrift in their reflections.

Upon entering the home, I found Cori, the wife, and Amanda, their daughter, in the living room. Though they were in the same space, they sat distanced from each other, both casting long, somber gazes down the hallway. The heavy, anguished sobs of the father echoed from a bedroom, filling the air with the unmistakable sound of grief. In my brief conversation with Cori, her profound worry for Jeff, her husband, prevented her from coming to terms with her emotions.

The police sergeant pulled me aside, providing a clearer picture of the unfolding events. He stressed the urgency of speaking with Jeff, but the man had separated himself in the bedroom since the harrowing moment he discovered his son after hearing the gunshot.

He explained how the father had hidden under the covers, including his head, and was now entirely out of sight, refusing to talk to anyone. The sergeant's requests to come out from under the covers had no effect. Finally, the sergeant asked if I could do anything to help. Entering the bedroom, I could see the covers shake as he wept. Once again, I found myself in a situation where it was difficult to find the right words. Even trying to find a starting point was elusive. Instead of attempting to start a conversation, I prayed for help to surface. Yet, my mind remained blank. I had nothing, so settling onto the floor, with my back against the wall, I let him know, "There's someone here with you."

That is all I said for a while, as I continued racking my mind for meaningful words, then I heard:

"Are you still here?"

"Yes."

"Who are you?"

"Jim, I'm a chaplain with the police."

"Go away!"

"I am just here to help."

"I don't need any help!"

"You are hiding in your bed with the covers pulled over your head. Would you like to rephrase that?"

"You have no idea!"

"You are right. I don't know what you are experiencing, but I am familiar with the pain of suicide in a family. So I care about what you are going through."

The covers were open just enough to frame his face, and he said, "I am sorry."

"A tragedy like this is difficult for anyone to process."

"Why did he do this?"

I did not attempt to answer the question but responded, "That is a question you may never get answered.

The police have some questions they need to ask you. Would it be possible for the sergeant to talk to you now? It might feel like they're just doing their job, but they care. The sergeant asked me to meet with you first and give you some space and support before he got into his questions."

"Will you stay when he comes in?" he asked. His question was unexpected. We had just met, yet somehow, my presence at this moment offered comfort. I remained sitting on the floor, hoping my silent empathy was palpable. Reflecting later, I wondered if my calm demeanor when he first saw me had forged an unspoken bond.

"Could I bring in the sergeant now?" I inquired.

"Let's just get this over with," Jeff responded.

I signaled the sergeant, who was waiting in the hallway. He entered and began relentless questioning, trying to get answers to questions where there were none. Jeff remained beneath the covers this entire time, his face the only visible part of him. I stayed seated on the floor, a silent witness, until the sergeant's departure.

Then, broaching the subject, "Jeff, Cori's in the living room. She's facing this too. May I bring her in?"

"Yes."

I escorted Cori back to Jeff, sensing their need for private time together. I excused myself, saying, "I need to speak with the police," and closed the door behind me. Later, when we reconvened, the conversation centered on the essential decisions and arrangements they faced.

After the medical examiner finished, they prepared Mark's body for transportation to the coroner. I remained close to Jeff and Cori as they weathered a tumultuous sea of emotions. When they reminisced about Mark's younger years, their voices were tinged with pride as they shared memories. Amanda, however, remained silent. Their narrative shifted to more recent, troubled times, revealing conflicting perspectives about their

What Was I Missing?

son. The story of Mark's struggle unfolded in layers—it began with bullying, which spiraled into a descent into drug use as he sought escape from his pain.

The impact on the family was intense, almost tearing them apart. As I witnessed their profound grief, it wasn't easy hearing how complex their journey had been.

In time, our conversation shifted toward the immediate decisions needed for the funeral. Despite this focus, a nagging unease lingered in my mind, a sense that something crucial was being overlooked.

Then, my pager beeped with a new call. I saw this as an opportunity to step back and return in a couple of days. I hoped the distance in time would clarify my unsettled thoughts. As the day wound down, I realized there had been no significant interaction between Jeff, Cori, and their daughter. It was a sobering insight. In the aftermath of tragedy, while one might expect families to come together in shared grief, the reality is often more complicated. Individuals can become trapped in emotional turmoil, and the instinct to support each other might not be immediate.

The following day, I made an unannounced visit. They invited me in, but their posture hinted at my intrusion. Jeff and his wife settled on the couch in the living room while their daughter took a distant chair, and I sat opposite the daughter. The space between the parents and the daughter felt more significant than just the ten-foot gap.

I started a discussion with Jeff, attempting to steer our dialogue toward his job and other neutral subjects before addressing the real reason I came back. He responded, but seemed reluctant to open up. I intended to keep him engaged, hoping to encourage him to acknowledge his grief and to avoid retreating into an emotional shell.

At one point, he said, "I know what you are doing." This comment let me know I was out of time and he wanted me to leave.

"What is that?"

"You are trying to distract me."

"No, I don't think that is possible."

"Then you are trying to see if I am okay."

"That is closer."

Glancing toward their daughter, who had remained silent throughout my visit, I couldn't help but notice the interplay of fear and confusion in her eyes. She sat quietly, her gaze fixed on the flickering flames in the fireplace. Her body language told me Amanda was experiencing thoughts and feelings unvoiced, perhaps intimidated by the weight of the surrounding conversation or unable to find the right words to express her thoughts.

"I know that your being 'okay' will continue to be a challenge. The reason behind my coming back to have this conversation and asking you these questions is not so that I can see if you will be okay."

I gestured toward Amanda, then continued, "She, more than me, needs to know you will be okay." Then, Jeff and his daughter looked at each other for the first time in my presence. With tears running down her face, Amanda stood up, as did her dad, sobbing, and they connected as they held onto each other.

Not wanting to interrupt, I stood up and headed for the door.

Cori smiled as I passed by and mouthed, "Thank you." Then leaving I closed the front door.

Two Weeks Later

It is rare to receive a request to return after something like this. So many stimuli can trigger terrible memories. As chaplains, we often find ourselves at the forefront of that list after becoming involved with families during their rawest moments of grief and vulnerability. So, it was a surprise to have Jeff ask if I had time for a cup of coffee.

When I got there, the whole family was sitting at the table. Jeff started by apologizing for how he acted the day after his son's death. He said he had realized I cared about his family after his anger had passed.

We sat around the kitchen table and discussed their grief, pain, and expected recovery time. Yet I sensed their more profound need might have been to talk with someone familiar with the impact of suicide.

"It will never disappear," I began. "Many people describe it as adjusting to a 'new normal.' Expecting things to return to how they once were isn't realistic."

Jeff hesitated, then admitted, "My anger's overwhelming. I fluctuate between grief and a fierce resentment for the turmoil he's brought into our lives again. Why didn't he approach me? We could've worked through this together."

"There are aspects you may never understand," I shared.

"My anger is reshaping my interactions with family and friends. I am finding myself lashing out over nothing."

Both his wife and daughter gave affirming nods at this.

Jeff inquired, "Do you have any advice?" His voice was edged with desperation.

"I'm not a therapist, but seeking counseling seems logical, and it might benefit all of you to go together. Often, families find that they're grappling with shared emotions and challenges. Facing them together can foster unity."

"Any other suggestions?"

"Would you be open to hearing a story about another father who struggled with anger after a similar experience?"

Jeff's face tightened. "I'm not in the mood to hear about someone else's issues."

Cori interjected, "What if it might help, Jeff?"

I offered, "Remember, the complexities of your son's journey and his decisions might forever remain a mystery."

Jeff looked at Cori and Amanda and permitted me to share about the letter with him.

Al's Letter

I recalled an incident involving another father following the same type of tragedy. While each situation has unique challenges, Grady's father's approach to his anger stood out for how he addressed it creatively. It's vital to note that this father, Al, grappled with an overpowering anger. The transformation became so bleak that friends distanced themselves and avoided hanging out with him.

Al was the father and Grady the son who took his own life—leaving behind his sister, Julie, and mother, Judy.

While planning Grady's memorial service Al confided in me about many of his regrets, and words he wished he'd shared with his son but now never could. He could not stop thinking about missing those opportunities.

More than a few storms had marked Grady's life after high school, where he found himself in rehab multiple times, and his addiction led him to steal from his family to fuel his habits. For his father, anger wasn't just an emotion: it threatened to overshadow his ability to grieve. He would return to past events, emphasizing the impact of Grady's problems on the family. Through it all, his wife called him selfish.

As I watched Jeff's reaction while I talked, I was worried he might shut me down at any time because the issues that had affected Al were very similar to his own experience.

I recalled a spontaneous thought that had developed one day in a discussion with Al. "I wonder if you would consider writing a letter to Grady?" Even now, I firmly believe that idea originated from the Holy Spirit. In retrospect, it seemed like the sincerest means of communication I could think of. The reflection required to compose such a letter might be healing.

I felt honored to speak at Grady's memorial service a few weeks later. As I concluded my remarks, I invited attendees to share their memories of Grady. What happened next was something I could not have expected.

Al, who had kept to himself most of the day, stepped forward while carrying a metal trash can and asked everyone to pause before they shared. He approached the microphone and pulled a sealed envelope from inside his coat. As he broke the seal and started reading, the torrent of raw emotions that followed shocked everyone. For an intense twenty minutes, Al laid bare the extent of the turmoil his family endured because of Grady's addiction. He spoke of vehicular crashes, substance abuse, unresolved family wounds, persistent disappointments, and the emotional scars Grady had etched into their lives. As Al's narrative progressed, he spoke of the resentment and blame that infected his heart, a bitterness directed at Grady for all the havoc he had caused.

The intensity of Al's emotions gripped everyone in the room. His words were so charged with pain and anger that I had to divert my eyes. The atmosphere was heavy. The hush over the room was so profound that even his closest friends were no longer looking at him.

As he continued to read, his daughter and wife glanced at me, their eyes conveying unspoken blame: *This was your idea. You suggested he write the letter.* I shared their sentiment. What had I done? I hadn't considered a reaction this powerful.

His words brimmed with intense anger throughout his sharing, and by the time he concluded, that intensity hadn't diminished. I had never witnessed something like this. We were here to celebrate Grady's life, and hearing this from the father was unsettling.

As Al neared the conclusion of the nine-page letter, he lifted the metal trash can he'd brought forward and set it on the table next to the podium, so it sat before him. We all wondered what he was doing, but no one could see this coming.

What Was I Missing?

Lifting his gaze as if communicating with Grady, he said, emphasizing each word, "Grady, I will always love you, and I forgive you. Please forgive me." Then he set the letter on fire, holding on to it until the last moment and letting the ashes fall into the waste can. Without another word, he hurried from the room. Unaware of Al's plan, his wife and daughter ran after him.

When the family returned, a visible transformation had taken place in Al. The weight of the years, the burden of anger, seemed to have lifted. There was a renewed lightness in his demeanor.

When I shared this event with Jeff, he took a moment to process it. After that, our conversation meandered. Al's story faded into the background as we chatted about various topics and questions. However, Jeff stopped me at the door as I was about to leave. He told me that Al's story and letter had affected him; it was an experience he hoped to have for himself soon.

Insights

Reflecting on the calls where someone has ended their life, there are commonalities I've observed and tried to impart to the survivors. There isn't a one-size-fits-all chart to guide us. Everyone navigates this storm differently, finding their rhythm and pace in processing their grief and making sense of the unthinkable.

- Survivors need to give themselves grace and room during this time. The whirlwind of emotions is confusing. It's not uncommon to oscillate between anger at their loved one for making that choice and the crippling self-blame that sometimes follows. The path to understanding and healing isn't linear; acknowledging this is often the first step toward acceptance.

- These are only a few of the thoughts that often race through the minds of survivors:

    - ☐ How did I not see the signs?
    - ☐ Is it my fault?
    - ☐ How could they leave us like this?
    - ☐ Why am I thinking of myself right now?
    - ☐ Did I overlook apparent hints?
    - ☐ Did I push them to this point?

- The overwhelming aspect behind these thoughts is how they surge together. It becomes challenging for survivors to untangle their emotions when each thought intersects and muddles the next, creating a storm of feelings. I'd notice survivors clutching their phones, lost in thought, paralyzed about whom to call or what step to take next. In such moments, I'd suggest holding off on making immediate calls and allowing us time to chat. People typically responded to this proposal with an exhale of gratitude. Though they yearn for the support of loved ones, the thought of recounting the tragedy, of finding the words to convey the news, is formidable. Repeating the painful narrative, delving into the details with each new person, becomes an excruciating task. From my experience, the simple phrase, "[Name] has taken their own life," is often all that's required. It conveys the gravity without necessitating further elaboration. In addition, since it doesn't require the use of the word suicide, it is easier to repeat.

- Another thing I often share with survivors is an understanding regarding the absence of timely calls from close friends. Just because someone hasn't reached out doesn't show a lack of concern. The reality is the weight of a suicide can leave many at a loss for words. They might hesitate, fearing their comments intensify the pain and thus delay the call. This delay can spiral into guilt as time passes, making the eventual call seem even more daunting. If survivors mention a close friend they haven't heard from, I often advise them to take the initiative. Reach out and invite that friend over. Sometimes, it's about bridging that gap of silence, which can make a world of difference for both sides.

Reflections on the Holy Spirit

In the stillness that followed the upheaval, a profound lesson took shape, one both unexpected and enlightening: the essence of maintaining faith and seeking the Holy Spirit's intervention. The wisdom to leave and return the next day wasn't mine but was a gift from beyond my realm of situational awareness. Missing the subtle cues of the daughter's lack of participation during the conversations seemed like a failing. Yet what began as an oversight became a blessing in disguise. It wasn't until I had left the scene that I recognized the value of what I had overlooked. This missed sign became

What Was I Missing?

a pivotal moment of grace, allowing me to see the Spirit's timing. It taught me that sometimes, what we perceive as mistakes can guide us to where we need to be, offering more profound help than we could have imagined.

I credit help that appeared at just the right time, like the letter, to the Holy Spirit.

CHAPTER 14

I'm Fine, Really I'm Fine, Thanks for Asking—PTSD

> If you give it to God, He transforms your test into a testimony, your mess into a message, and your misery into a ministry.
>
> —RICK WARREN

Have you ever wondered what PTSD looks like? For me, it looked like this.

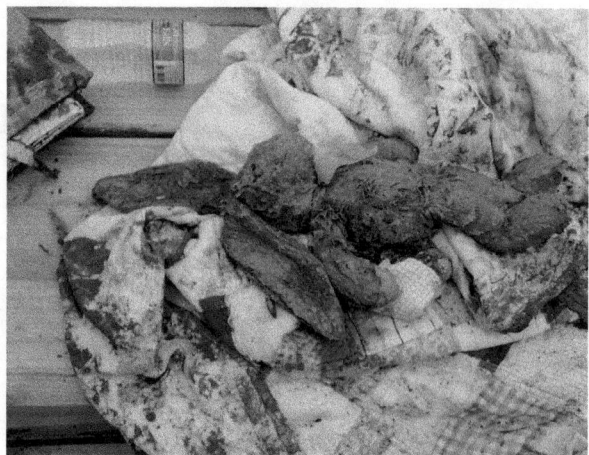

Recovered by the National Guard searchers at Oso Mud Slide

It was a mudslide where forty-three people lost their lives that day. They represented so many people living along the river in this small community. For the first three days, I was with the families and survivors at the location that the Red Cross had set up in a middle school. Then, they requested me to go to the "pile," which became the term used for the mudslide site. For the next twenty-three days, I would arrive around 7:00 a.m. to help in any way possible. I began by moving from group to group to see how they were doing and thank them for their help.

Somehow, I found myself a spotter on a large track hoe, watching the buckets of mud and the surrounding area for victims. I don't remember exactly why, but I got involved in searching by hand alongside volunteers, first responders, and National Guard personnel to help locate remains, getting stuck waist-deep twice and needing help to be pulled out of the mud.

On my first day at the pile, while waiting my turn to go through the decontamination process and get hosed down, I spotted four searchers from the National Guard approaching. Each held a corner of what turned out to be a homemade quilt, carrying it like a stretcher. They set the quilt down just a few feet from where we stood. It was off to the side but in full view of the searchers waiting to get sprayed down. Everyone would have to walk just feet from the quilt and what its contents represented. Once they set the quilt down, the National Guard personnel headed off to join the end of the line. I noticed that the conversations that were going on abruptly stopped as the searchers stared at the muddy, pink bunny rabbit with long, floppy ears.

Stepping out of the line, I went to where they had gently laid the bunny down, treating it with the utmost respect as if it were a human casualty. Kneeling in the mud, I folded the quilt with reverence and care, ensuring the bunny was entirely out of view. Just as I had finished, one of the four individuals who had rescued the pink bunny came rushing back, demanding to know what I was doing. Rather than looking up or making eye contact, I quietly suggested that he slowly turn around and look at the people waiting to get decontaminated. With empathy, I expressed my gratitude for the care they had shown bringing the bunny here. Still, I couldn't ignore that we were all grappling with intense emotions at that moment, and the sight of the muddy, stuffed companion served as a poignant reminder of the missing child.

His response was wordless; he simply nodded and slowly walked away after a few moments. Then, picking up and carrying the quilt containing the pink bunny, I moved it out of the sight of everyone in the line, hoping to remove a trigger for the overwhelming grief they shared.

Easter came a few weeks later. Stuffed bunny rabbits started showing up in stores about a week after the slide happened. I remained on site of the slide until a few days after Easter. Ever since that day, stuffed bunny rabbits and helicopters have been a trigger for me.

In our world, various diseases lurk, some of which people may overlook or deem harmless, while others inflict physical or mental harm. It's possible to experience Post-Traumatic Stress Disorder, commonly known as PTSD, after exposure to something that profoundly affects the body or experiencing a situation so upsetting that words cannot capture its magnitude.

But what precisely is PTSD? It is a disorder that affects individuals who have undergone traumatic events. In such circumstances, it is normal for individuals to experience significant effects during and after the ordeal. The automatic response to fear can trigger physiological changes, rapidly preparing us to confront or escape danger, known as the fight-or-flight response. This response aims to safeguard us from harm during frightening encounters.

Trauma leads to various reactions in individuals. However, for those who continue to grapple with lingering issues, the sense of stress and fear may persist even when they are no longer in immediate danger, filtering their perception of the world around them.

PTSD can be a formidable and persistent adversary, leaving those affected constantly vigilant and apprehensive. Understanding and empathizing with those who endure this condition can be crucial in supporting their journey toward healing and recovery.

Besides experiencing trauma firsthand, we need to acknowledge that witnessing traumatic events, even from a distance or without being directly in harm's way, can also profoundly affect an individual's mental and emotional well being.

After witnessing distressing scenes, such as natural disasters, accidents, acts of violence, or the suffering of others, individuals may still experience profound emotional impact. This phenomenon is sometimes called *vicarious trauma* or *secondary trauma*.

Repeated exposure to traumatic stories, images, or events through media, one's profession, or proximity to others who have endured traumatic experiences can lead to vicarious trauma in individuals. The constant

I'm Fine, Really I'm Fine, Thanks for Asking—PTSD

influx of distressing information can internalize others' pain and suffering, resulting in emotional exhaustion, feelings of helplessness, and a heightened sense of vulnerability.

People working in professions like healthcare, emergency response, law enforcement, or journalism are susceptible to vicarious trauma because of their work. However, it can affect anyone who encounters distressing content or has close connections with individuals who have experienced trauma.

Recognizing the potential effects of witnessing traumatic events is crucial in understanding the complexities of post-traumatic stress and its diverse signs. For those grappling with vicarious trauma, seeking support, counseling, or peer debriefing can help to process these emotions and mitigate the long-term effects.

Just as we show empathy and understanding to those directly affected by trauma, extending the same compassion to those who have witnessed such events indirectly is essential in fostering a supportive and healing environment for all.

One day, I was having coffee with one of the battalion chiefs when he asked me to create a PTSD presentation. This request was a surprise. I knew the battalion chief might have his reasons; still, I wished to learn the reason behind his plea. He explained that his crew had been on several tough calls in the last month. Then, after those calls, he had two personnel come to him individually and talk to him privately, "off the record," about different calls.

I asked the BC what he had in mind. He said having a presentation before one of the training exercises would be helpful and might make the topic safe to bring up later. Maybe spend fifteen minutes to help them be more open to discussing what they might have experienced during horrifying scenes. I responded, "Chief, they usually take that much time just to get coffee and sit down. If they have questions, can I extend the session?"

He laughed, saying, "I know it will be challenging, but just try your best, and I know you will do a good job." Those words created excitement for this opportunity. Still, I wondered what I could say in fifteen minutes to make a lasting impression beyond this meeting. Because, if they listen to me and don't fully understand the potential impact of PTSD, I might not have another opportunity to address this unspoken issue.

Later, while sitting on my deck wondering how to approach this topic, I watched my grandkids. They had come over and were playing in the backyard. We had just experienced a windstorm, with branches and debris all over the yard. Watching them work together, taking turns pulling a wagon around the yard and picking up fallen branches of trees and pinecones, provided an unexpected answer. They had the branches piled high in the wagon to where it would stop the wagon when they tried to run over a rock or another stick on the ground.

That was when I realized my grandkids were giving me the answer: They had no trouble overcoming the obstacles when the wagon was not full. They understood that when they began struggling to pull the wagon, it was time to empty it and start again.

While researching, I visited the stations and sat down for coffee with some firefighters. I mentioned I had the challenge of preparing a presentation for the stations. I wondered what they would like to know. Their answer surprised me. "We don't know what you do." Thinking about their response, it made sense to me.

Arriving at the scene, I often found the medics already gone or in the process of leaving. Their swift departure signaled a grim outcome for their patients and why I was there. My role was primarily to offer support to grieving families, but beyond that, the first responders knew little about what chaplains did. Once their medical skills were no longer required, they would leave promptly, perhaps hoping to avoid the emotional burden of facing the families and experiencing further empathy for them.

Surprisingly, even after having chaplains serving in the area for decades, there seemed to be a significant gap in understanding our role. I had assumed that the firefighters, with their extensive experience in emergencies, would be familiar with our responsibilities when we responded to scenes. Their response revealed a lack of awareness about the support we provided to the families and victims after they left.

This realization highlighted the need for better communication and collaboration between first responders and chaplains. While the medics focused on saving lives and providing medical care, our mission as chaplains was to offer support, compassion, and a comforting presence to the bereaved. By bridging this information gap, we could foster a more cohesive and empathetic approach to assisting those affected by tragic events.

I was explaining what we try to accomplish when talking with families or victims when a firefighter asked what happened after a specific call. He described the family attempting to jog my memory because I was the chaplain there that day. I reflected on the emotional and challenging incident. The scene was hauntingly somber, with the medics having departed shortly after my arrival. It was heartbreaking when I responded to a call involving a teenager who had tragically taken her own life.

The weight of such situations is indescribable, and the aftermath of such a devastating event profoundly affects everyone involved. As a chaplain, I provided support and comfort to the grieving family and others grappling with immense pain and loss. During the tragedy, I offered a compassionate presence to those shattered by sorrow.

Though the medics had left the scene, my duty to the affected individuals remained unwavering. I committed myself fully to supporting the emotional well being of the family and friends who needed to navigate the aftermath of these heart-wrenching incidents. Together, we mourned the life lost too soon, attempting to make sense of an unfathomable tragedy.

Additional firefighters in the room joined us. This shift was the one who responded that day. I told them what I had shared with the family. We equipped them with resources and gave them a briefing on what occurred in the days that followed. I was aware of the firefighter who had asked about the girl's family sinking back into his chair. Hearing what had happened after they left gave him closure. Immediately, someone else asked about another call. Before I could answer all their questions, the alarm tones went off, and they headed out to a traffic accident.

I decided to visit the other stations, asking the same question. "What might be helpful for you to know?" Their answers were similar—"We don't know what you do"—opening great conversations.

With the time constraint involved, I felt it might be best to acknowledge that PTSD exists, be aware of it, and have a way to acknowledge it.

Short Version of the PTSD Presentation: Understanding the Impact and Coping Strategies

Introduction: Hello everyone! Today, I'd like to share a simple analogy that might provide a new perspective on the challenges of PTSD and how it can accumulate. Imagine a little red wagon, like the ones kids used to have, and visualize pulling it down a dirt road with a few small potholes and stones.

Encountering rocks and stones: In your journey as first responders, you may come across situations that are difficult to forget. Those events become the rocks on your path. To keep moving, you may start placing these stones in the wagon, seemingly not realizing their weight and impact on your emotional well being.

The accumulative effect: As time passes, the wagon feels heavier as you encounter new obstacles. It takes more effort to get back on the level part of the road, representing the challenges of coping with cumulative stress.

Exploring options: Now, let's consider some options to lighten the load and cope with the cumulative effect of PTSD:

1. Dump the wagon: While you can attempt to unload everything simultaneously, the weight may be overwhelming. Seeking support from peers or professionals is essential.
2. Remove a few rocks: Gradually remove some emotional burdens, ensuring not to add them back excessively. Practicing self-care and seeking help when needed is vital.
3. Get a larger wagon: This represents the risky attempt to build additional self-resilience and coping mechanisms to delay addressing the problem. You are fooling yourself if you think you can handle significant stressors more effectively. Adopting this strategy, you will still need help to pull or dispose of its contents.

Conclusion: As first responders, it's crucial to acknowledge our emotional weight and the potential cumulative impact of PTSD. By addressing our mental health and supporting each other, we can ensure that we continue to walk down the road of resilience and well being. Remember, taking care of your wagon can make all the difference.

Thank you for your time.

The feedback I received told me that what I had shared was so simple it gave them a different way to acknowledge the problems of PTSD and understand that there can be a cumulative effect.

Two weeks later, while visiting some friends, we walked by a park and saw this two-story little red wagon. I made a copy of the picture and gave it to the BC. After that, I noticed he posted it on the wall in the dayroom as a reminder. It was there for a while, and he said it had opened up a few discussions. They asked each other how their wagon was doing after hard calls.

Two-story red wagon at Spokane's Riverfront Park

Mudslide Insights

For me, the breakthrough came five years after the mudslide. Until then, just hearing helicopters could sometimes remind me of the first days at the pile. Then, the only way to remove remains was for helicopters to hover and lower a basket by cable to retrieve them. Having one fly low near me was enough to cause me to walk off a golf course months later. I had no desire to drive to my favorite fishing spot. I avoided driving the road to the river. This highway went through the middle of the slide area. I knew the survivors had a memorial service every year on the anniversary of the slide, but I could not bring myself to go.

The last time I saw most of these people, we were at the middle school with the Red Cross. None of those who had been there had any idea why I had not returned to the school or knew that I had spent the following weeks searching for the remains of their families. It was chaos that first night while talking with a man who had gone to town to get some part to fix something for his uncle's home. He told me he had served two tours in Iraq while in the army. Then I heard two young women behind me state, "They're dead. Our parents are dead." There was no emotion in their words. After hearing that, I asked the soldier if I could return to him later. His answer was, "Of course." He had also listened to the sisters. I looked for him after that but never found him. It was not until later that I learned he had taken his own life. I had difficulty moving on from the heartaches I saw that long day and night. Or from the guilt of not being able to help the soldier.

On the fifth anniversary, I stood at the back of the group, unsure if I should have come. Then I saw a man who had lost so much the day of the slide, and he was smiling and hugging the others who had come to the memorial service.

Watching him changed everything for me. In my mind, I was still at Post Middle School where the families were suffering or out on the pile recovering their loved ones. Seeing for myself that they were rebounding from their grief immediately helped me.

This experience is now helping me help others who experience PTSD.

CHAPTER 15

What Would You Say or Do?

Let your conversation be gracious and attractive so that you will have the right response for everyone.

—Col 4:6 NLT

IMAGINE YOURSELF AT A crossroads, faced with a choice that could bring solace to a grieving heart or leave words unspoken in the silence of loss. What would you do in these moments? The decisions are never easy, but they define our capacity for compassion. In this chapter I invite you to experience times when reaching out was additionally challenging.

Situation One

I responded to a scene marked by an unexpected loss: a husband and father had suddenly passed away, leaving his family in a state of shock and sorrow. As I entered the house, someone directed me to the front room where the family had gathered. The wife and her two sons, their wives, and an unmarried daughter were present. In another room, a stark reminder of the tragedy awaited—the husband, whom medics had unsuccessfully attended to.

The quietness of the room was striking as I walked in. It wasn't just the silence of mourning; it was as if the air was heavy with unspoken emotions. Though seated together, the family seemed worlds apart. Each lost in their reflections. The wife briefly met my gaze, her eyes a mirror of the emotions she was battling within.

What caught my attention next was the unusual array of lifelike dolls that filled the room. These weren't ordinary dolls; they were over three feet tall, meticulously crafted with glass eyes and realistic skin textures. They seemed to occupy the room with an almost tangible presence. Each doll was unique. Some even held more petite dolls, while others had miniature pets. Their lifelike appearances made the room unusually crowded, adding a surreal element to the mourning atmosphere.

One distinct girl doll sat on the coffee table just a few feet from where I sat. She was especially striking. She sat positioned in such a way that it was impossible to avoid her stare. The dolls seemed to hold a special place in the wife's life. However, I guessed that their presence could contribute to the silence and cause the averted gazes of the family members, particularly the daughter. Their discomfort, perhaps mingled with embarrassment, was apparent in their body language.

At that moment, I realized that not acknowledging the dolls would impede my time here. The room's unique dynamics, dominated by these silent, lifelike figures, posed a challenge. While a source of comfort or significance to the wife, the dolls seemed to act as an unspoken barrier in the room. To support this family effectively, I recognized I needed to not only address their grief but also acknowledge these dolls subtly. In doing so, I hoped to guide them gently toward a space where they could open up about their loss, share their feelings, and start grieving.

> Now, consider what you would say or do before reading on.

As I sat among the family, enveloped in a heavy silence, my mind considered how to reach out for a way to bridge the gap. Looking around the room filled with dolls, I wondered about their impact on the family. Should I acknowledge them, or would ignoring them seem overly polite and create a barrier between us? I considered whether addressing the dolls might help put the family at ease and foster a more comfortable atmosphere. My concern was the family might think I was insincere if I appeared too enthusiastic about the dolls. I intended to acknowledge their presence briefly and then focus on how I could help.

So I offered, "I feel like I am in a staring contest." This odd question caught the children off guard, sparking an unexpected wave of laughter. It began with hesitant giggles and grew into a hearty, infectious laughter that seemed to wash over us, bringing tears dangerously close to the surface. The sheer magnitude of their response hinted at how long it had been since someone had engaged with their world in such a lighthearted way. Even the wife, weighed down by her grief, momentarily felt lifted by the joy, offering her a fleeting escape from her sorrow. It was a reminder of the power of a simple, unexpected moment to bring light into the darkest of times.

Their reaction encouraged me to follow up with a more sincere inquiry. "These dolls are amazing. How did you come to collect them?" The wife, finding comfort in the subject, explained the origin of her collection. Each doll had its own story, and as she shared these, the children joined in. They shared about the different dolls, and their comfort with me increased.

The room's mood subtly shifted. What began as a moment of lightheartedness slowly developed into a warm conversation. The family's engagement with the dolls seemed to ease the tension, allowing them to step away from their grief, if only for a moment.

I gently nudged the conversation toward memories of their father and husband. They shared snippets of their life with him, each memory a small tribute to the man they were mourning. The atmosphere remained somber, but it was now interspersed with moments of fond remembrance.

By acknowledging the dolls and then gently transitioning to their shared memories, I created a space where the family could feel more at ease expressing themselves and finding comfort in the familiarity of their stories.

Situation Two

I arrived at the scene where a man's wife had passed away less than an hour before. From the driveway, I could see the husband working at a computer. It seemed somewhat strange to have a computer in the garage. However, the rest of the space contained various items that created a man cave. I checked in with the sheriff, who went forward to let the husband know I was there.

I remained outside in the driveway, trying to respect their privacy. The garage door was open, and their conversation was out of earshot, their voices muffled by the distance and the idling vehicles around us. From my vantage point, I could only see the husband's back, his posture rigid and tense. In a calm and respectful manner, the deputy informed him about my presence as a chaplain and my intention to provide support.

Suddenly, the husband's body language changed as he waved his hands animatedly. Even without hearing the words, I knew he did not want my involvement. During this time, he did not turn around or look at me.

After a short time, the deputy came back to me with an apologetic look on his face. He relayed the husband wanted me to leave. When I had arrived intending to offer support and resources, I recognized and respected his response. Given that he did not know what help I could provide, my presence might have seemed intrusive or unnecessary to him at that moment.

Would you leave or do something else?

As I stood with the sheriff on the sidewalk, I couldn't help but feel a sense of helplessness for the husband. My wife's father was Ukrainian and very stubborn, so learning he was Ukrainian encouraged me not to walk away without trying again. It was a solemn reminder of the delicate balance between offering support and respecting an individual's way of coping with loss.

Turning to the sheriff, I offered understandingly, "No problem, but could I have a quick word with the husband before I leave?" The sheriff hesitated for a moment before responding. His reply was tentative. "Well, it's probably not the best idea you have had, but if you really want to, go ahead." His tone and the look in his eyes reminded me of when my wife tells me, "Go ahead." It wasn't so much an approval as a challenge, almost as if she dared me to try.

I cautiously approached the Ukrainian man, who was busy at his computer in the garage, and as I got closer I saw he was sending out emails. Stopping to his right, I introduced myself softly as the chaplain, trying not to intrude too much into his space. Leaning slightly, I spoke in a low, reassuring tone, letting him know why I was there.

Yuri paused what he was doing and looked up, his eyes holding mine for a moment. It felt like he was trying to read my intentions to see if I was genuine. After a long silence, saying nothing, Yuri stood up, walked across the garage, and returned with a folding chair. Placing it beside his own, he motioned for me to sit down.

For the next three hours, we talked. It wasn't deep discussions but more about everyday things, Yuri's needs, and how I could help. I shared information about local resources and contacts within the Ukrainian community, hoping to connect him with people who could offer support in his native language. Our conversation was simple but meaningful, filled with pauses and nods, a shared understanding slowly forming between us.

The evening drew on, and the medical examiner still hadn't arrived. I was preparing to leave and standing to reach for a business card in my wallet.

Yuri unexpectedly stood and asked if I would say a prayer for his wife. We both stood, and I offered a brief, heartfelt prayer. Then, he surprised me again by giving me a bear hug. It was a warm, genuine gesture that spoke volumes.

Heading to my car, the deputy stopped me, asking, "What did you say?" I smiled and then shared, "I'm not here to save you. I'm not here to convert you, and I'm not here to pray if you don't want me to. I'm here to assist you in any way you need. I may have some resources that might help. Sometimes, it's not about the grand gestures but just being there, listening, and showing that I genuinely care."

This experience was a reminder that in times of loss, people don't always seek spiritual guidance, but they will look for a human connection, understanding, and a bit of practical help.

Situation Three

The fire scene was a stark reminder of how quickly life can change. With its unique trilevel design, the house had a bedroom directly above the garage. It was in the garage that the fire had started, rapidly engulfing both the garage and the main bedroom above. The loss devastated the homeowner, who ran a home gemstone business from here. He estimated about $200,000 worth of semiprecious gemstones, used for collections and jewelry making, had been on the wooden shelves in the garage. Now, the scene was one of utter chaos. Shelves that once held precious stones had collapsed during the fire or when the firefighters did the overhaul, scattering the rocks and gems amidst debris and ashes.

The husband and wife, who were already awake at the time of the fire and packed for a follow-up trip to the Mayo Clinic, instead watched their home and livelihood consumed by flames. They had been ready to leave, their bags by the front door at 5:00 a.m., only to have their plans derailed by the smoke emerging in their bedroom. The husband's worry about his disrupted business and the extensive damage to their home was substantial.

Feeling a tug of empathy the next day, I stopped by their house after church. The damage was evident, particularly in the bedroom and garage. The owners were sifting through what remained in the middle of wreckage and soot. They were searching for the gemstones that were now scattered throughout the debris from the fire. This scene of them rummaging through the remnants of their garage struck a chord with me. It was a mix of hope and resilience against loss and uncertainty.

As they moved through the debris with a sense of purpose, each recovered stone was a minor victory against the overwhelming loss. Watching them reminded me of the resilience of the human spirit in the face of adversity. Their determination to salvage something from the ashes was both inspiring and heartrending.

Walking up to them in the garage, I made sure they knew I was there for more than just the fire they had faced last night. I wanted them to feel that I cared about what they were going through. Their situation revealed how life could throw unexpected things at us and how tough people must be to pick up the pieces after something like this.

What would you say?

Something unexpected came to my mind. "I think you may have been blessed." They both stopped searching and looked at me like I was crazy. Then I gestured with my hand to include everything in the garage and added, "This is all just stuff, but I understand you have a monumental task of recovering your inventory and that it is quite a job." Putting a hand on both their shoulders as I looked at them. "You still have each other. As hard as it is to go through something like this, you still have each other. Had you not gotten up early to catch a flight to the clinic, there is an excellent chance that neither of you would have survived. It is why I think that you may have been blessed." They faced each other, and I think they realized what I had just said, and the tears flowed. The next thing I knew, they were both hugging each other. I excused myself and went back to my car. My wife had been watching all this through the window. She told me she wasn't sure what I had just said, but she saw the couple hugging and crying as I walked away.

Sometimes a change in perspective can make a big difference: I later found out that their story about the fire now emphasized what was saved rather than what was lost.

Situation Four

Arriving at the scene, I encountered an unexpected silence. Julie, the sister of the deceased, was there, her presence marked by a sense of shock. Her two daughters, Erin, eight, and Peggy, eleven, accompanied her. Earlier that day, Julie had grown increasingly worried after her attempts to reach her brother, Craig, went unanswered. Driven by concern, she visited, only to discover him unresponsive on the kitchen floor, prompting her to call 911.

In the parking lot, Julie was pacing back and forth without direction. Her movements were erratic between shock and disbelief. The scene included two police officers and a team of paramedics. They all remained on standby as they awaited the medical examiner's arrival.

Upon noticing my arrival, one officer made a discreet gesture toward Julie. It was a request for help, an acknowledgment that her pain was beyond their capacity to comfort.

As I approached Julie, I introduced myself as a chaplain. She immediately expressed concern for her daughters, Erin and Peggy, remaining in her car. She looked at them worriedly and asked if I could speak to them. Julie explained he was very close to them and added this was their first exposure to someone dying.

How would you approach the children?

Heading to the car, I opened the door on the side of the girl who I thought might be the oldest. I kneeled by the open door, and I acknowledged what I saw.

"I can tell you love your uncle a lot. Do you think he knows that?" They didn't speak, just nodded their heads.

"He must have been special."

Peggy says, "He was."

"Did he make you laugh?"

Both smiled, and Erin told me he always made them laugh.

"How did he do that?"

Then, I had the privilege of hearing their stories about their Uncle Craig. As they relived those moments, the laughter returned. The telling of the stories often included using animated hand gestures. Waiting until each shared some of their favorite memories, I suggested those memories will always be there for them, but I suggested that writing down some of their favorite ones might be a good idea. My thought was if they did that, they would relive those times. I went back to Julie, their mom. She had heard the kids laughing only minutes after I kneeled by the car. She shared she did not think that would have been possible.

I then listened as she told me about her brother. He had a hard life. Early on, he was involved with alcohol and then later drugs. As a result, his marriage failed, and he lost custody of his children. He had gone through rehab twice, but went back to the drugs. However, she said he had remained sober and drug free for the last few months. Then she asked the tricky question. Was there any way I could find out if he was sober when he died? Responding that I would see if I could find out, I joined the police in Craig's apartment. Craig was still lying on the floor of the kitchen. As I looked around, I saw some mixing bowls, a blender, cooking utensils, and different ingredients scattered on the counters. I hoped to find something to support a positive response to her question.

What Would You Say or Do?

Would you answer her question? "Was he sober when he died?"

"Julie, this is my opinion. I don't believe he was under the influence of anything when he died." Then I explained he was making a meal requiring much preparation and ingredients. Cooking something like that is not a spur-of-the-moment decision. It is something you would look forward to. If he were under the influence, he would have been looking for a simple solution to his hunger. I considered I could be wrong. However, seeing the change in her physical posture and that she seemed to relax some was reassuring. She said I would never know how much that meant to her and asked if I would do the memorial service for him.

Situation Five

You arrive at the scene of an unattended death. You recognize the man and woman standing beside the car from a call three months ago. That was when their other brother had died from complications of an infection. This time, you are at the home of another sibling. Someone had discovered him dead thirty minutes earlier. Their father remains sitting in the car as he had at the previous call for his other son.

On the first call, the son and daughter had asked if I might talk to their dad about hearing aids. They had noticed I had them and shared that their dad would do nothing about his hearing problem. They described situations where it was challenging to communicate. It was hopeless whenever they wanted to spend time with him or have dinner at a restaurant. They had to yell, disturbing the others close by, to have any semblance of a conversation. I tried talking to him last time, but was unsure if he would follow up. Now, he has not moved his head to look at me and has continued to stare straight ahead with no emotion visible.

The son and daughter have asked me to try again. I can sense their frustration and sense of loss.

How would you respond to the son and daughter's request? First, consider how you can get his attention.

Their father, Bob, stared straight ahead as I stood beside the car. He was in the front right seat with the door open and holding on to something in his lap. I kneeled at his level and put my hand on his arm. Then he turned and looked at me. "Bob, we are not supposed to bury our children. So sorry we are meeting again like this." After I said that, his emotions came out, and he began sobbing, which had not happened before. I remained kneeling there until he could talk, and then I offered to help however I could. We continued to speak, and I helped again with calling the funeral home.

When I felt the timing was right, "Bob, remember when we talked about hearing aids?" I started, but as soon as the words left my mouth, I sensed his attention shutting down. I kept my hand reassuringly on his shoulder, trying to maintain a connection. "You know I use them?" His gaze returns to mine, a hint of surprise, shaking his head no. "I'm wearing them now." I pulled one out to show him its small size. "Most people don't even notice I have them on. With these, I can easily chat with my wife, kids, and grandkids without them needing to raise their voices. And I don't have to keep asking 'what?' as often. Also, movies are more enjoyable when they are not silent." That brought a hint of a smile; I had hoped to strike a chord with him. "I have been there, Bob. You've had moments where you smile and nod during conversations, pretending to understand rather than asking someone to repeat themselves. I used to do that a lot too. But since I started wearing hearing aids, those awkward situations happen less often. It would be a pity to miss out on enjoying the time you have left with your family. You know, Costco offers free hearing tests. They'll even let you try on a pair of hearing aids and walk around the store to test them. It made an incredible difference for me. Why not give it a try? There's nothing to lose, and the difference might surprise you." I knew his son and daughter were standing off to the side and slightly behind us, and could listen to my conversation with Bob without him seeing them.

Two weeks later, his son called me. They were at Costco, where his dad was walking around the store with his sister, and he told me both were smiling. This intervention may not have happened if God had not affected my hearing first, giving me firsthand experience with hearing loss.

CHAPTER 16

Teen Suicide Prevention

LifeWalk Presentation

EVERY DAY, THE TRAGEDY of suicide claims too many young lives that early intervention and better understanding might have saved.

This presentation is a resource developed after years of witnessing the devastating effects of untreated mental health issues. My goal is to provide a tool that empowers counselors, teachers, and parents to step into these crucial moments, not just as authority figures but as lifelines.

The challenge with some interventions is that they often feel clinical or detached from the realities teens face. LifeWalk is different. It's something simple, speaks their language, and has a lasting impact. The seed of the LifeWalk concept was planted while sitting on a curb with a father who had just lost his son to suicide; it developed later during conversations with my grandson. It goes beyond being a presentation; it combines powerful visuals and content designed to connect with young people in a way they will remember. More importantly, it equips them with tools to help themselves and support their friends.

Through this presentation, I want to offer more than just another resource. I want to provide hope through a practical strategy designed to create a way to make a difference. Whether you're a counselor, teacher, or parent, you hold the potential to change the course of someone's life. I hope this concept helps you to help them.

The Reality of Suicide

If you have ever watched a debate, you've likely concluded that 94 percent of all statistics are made up on the spot. We all know how numbers are manipulated to emphasize a point. It is essential not to take the facts about suicide lightly. I assure you, what I am about to share is based on hard truth, not conjecture.

In my time as a chaplain, I responded to over eighty suicides. But that number alone doesn't capture the full gravity of the issue. I was on call only about 20 percent of the time. The actual number of suicides in our community during those ten years was closer to four hundred. Let that sink in: four hundred families were devastated by suicide, and their lives are forever impacted.

A significant portion of these tragic cases involved teenagers. To me, these aren't just numbers. I was there. These are events where young people in our community felt overwhelmed and hopeless and saw no other option. The numbers underscore how crucial it is to recognize the signs, step in early, and offer the support these teens desperately need.

This isn't something happening "somewhere else." It's happening here to kids sitting in our classrooms, living in our neighborhoods, and sometimes even in our homes. If we don't act, we risk losing more of them. But we can save lives if we learn to recognize the warning signs.

The LifeWalk presentation is not just talking to kids; it's a visual way to impact them in a way that truly resonates. Too often, conversations about suicide feel distant, clinical, or difficult to grasp. But young people need more than statistics or lectures—they need something to connect with and can make a lasting impression.

What you're about to learn is a visual approach to discussing suicide that I have found to be influential and makes a difference. This isn't just information; it's a lifeline. By presenting these ideas visually, we engage kids in a way that sticks with them, opening their eyes to the seriousness of the issue while offering them the proper tools to navigate their struggles or to help a friend who may be struggling.

This presentation can help you, as a counselor, teacher, or parent, speak to the heart of the issue. Knowing means little if you can't pass it on. However, these critical conversations can lead to change when you have the information and a method to share it.

LifeWalk Presentation

There are four takeaways I want you to leave with today—four things that could make all the difference when reaching out to help a child or teenager who might be at risk of suicide.

But before we dive into those, could I share a personal story that explains what drives me to do this work? (Take a moment to make eye contact with everyone before continuing.)

My first suicide call came in 1997. (Use my story if you don't have your own.) Brad was a senior at Meadowdale High School. I arrived at the scene shortly after his brother found him. Brad had taken his own life with a gun. I can still picture the scene as if it were yesterday. Suicides are like that, and they leave a lasting impression. His father, two brothers, and his older brother's wife, Cori, were all there, along with three police officers. The weight of the moment was heavy, almost unbearable. None of Brad's family members said a word for five long hours. There were few tears, no shouts, just silence. It was a silence that spoke louder than anything else ever could.

I wanted so badly to offer comfort, to say something that might help ease their unimaginable pain. But I didn't know how. I didn't know what to say, and truthfully, I didn't know where to begin. Sometimes, silence can be more painful than words. To this day, over twenty-five years later, Brad's family still rarely talk about him. The grief and the pain are too much to bear, so they keep it locked away.

This experience deeply marked me. It taught me that these tragic situations affect individuals and leave entire families and communities grappling with the aftermath. It is why I'm here today. To prevent as many families as I can from enduring that silence, from carrying around the weight suicide brings.

In 2019, another tragedy struck close to home. A student from Hazelwood High School took his own life, and my daughter Cori was deeply affected because, in a conversation with Sam, her son, Cori asked him if he had ever had similar thoughts. What Sam shared next hit hard: he said that he sometimes thinks about his uncle Brad and suicide. The pain and silence that had hung over our family since Brad's death had left its mark on him also. His classmate's parents found a note. It read, "You will be better off without me."

That one sentence captures the heartbreaking loneliness and despair so many teens feel when they believe that ending their lives is the only way out.

If you haven't already pieced it together, Sam is my grandson, Cori is my daughter, and Brad is my son-in-law's brother. Sam was not born when Brad died, but that event still affected him. Hearing Sam talk about those dark thoughts shook me to my core. As much as I had tried to protect my family, I realized that even those closest to us are not immune to the darkness of suicide's shadow.

Thankfully, Sam is now twenty-three and doing well. But during that time, as I spoke with him, I noticed he struggled to maintain eye contact, often gazing off into the distance—a common response among teenagers. I realized I needed to find a way to help him focus on the real issue: the heartbreaking reality of a teenager taking their own life.

Simply discussing what had happened and how he felt wasn't enough. I needed to reach him on a deeper, more personal level—something visual and impactful. That's when I developed the LifeWalk concept, a tool designed to move beyond surface-level conversations and connect with teens like Sam, who struggle in silence.

This is why I'm so passionate about this presentation. It's not just a teaching tool—it's a means to build bridges of understanding and connection, offering hope and support before it's too late.

The Beginning

This part offers an analogy to help teens understand how everyone has unique roles and gifts.

Many teen suicides happen because someone feels like they don't measure up. They look at others and their achievements, appearance, and popularity and convince themselves they can't improve. But here's something to consider: why would a painter compare themselves to a musician? Or a sprinter to a marathon runner? They're all artists or athletes in their own right, but their talents and strengths are entirely different.

A painter doesn't need to play a song to create something beautiful, and a sprinter doesn't need to run twenty-six miles to be fast. Each has a unique role and skill set that makes them exceptional at what they do. So why do we spend so much time comparing ourselves to others when our paths and abilities differ entirely?

In sports, every player has a specific role. The quarterback and receiver have distinct skill sets, just as the center fielder's role differs from the catcher's. No one questions why players focus on what suits their position best—each is important. A team can't function unless every player does their part.

The same is true in other activities. In a choir, each voice has a part. In a band, each instrument plays a different role. Why is it easier for us not to envy someone else's talent in sports or music? Maybe it's because we understand everyone has their place in those—that each person's contribution is valuable, and no one can do it all.

The same principle applies to life. We all have different roles, unique talents, and different paths. It's when we recognize this that we can stop comparing ourselves to others and start appreciating the unique role we each play.

Imagine seeing ourselves and others that way—not as competitors, but as part of a larger team, each with a crucial role. That's when we understand that our worth isn't about comparing ourselves to someone else's talent or achievements. It's about realizing that our gifts matter too, and they're part of something bigger than ourselves.

Speaking to the kids, has anyone ever told you that you are uniquely created? I'm sure many of you have heard that, but I want to know if you believe it. Do you truly understand what that means?

I'll be honest—it took me a long time to grasp the total weight of that statement. It sounds simple, but its significance is life-changing if you can embrace it. It can completely alter how you see yourself and the world around you.

Takeaway One

Let me explain why this idea matters so much. If you agree that God has uniquely made you, this is also correct: God compares you to no one. Let that sink in for a moment. God doesn't hold you up next to anyone else. He doesn't measure your worth based on someone else's gifts or abilities. He made you exactly as you are and did it intentionally and purposefully.

There is incredible freedom in that knowledge. When you cease comparing yourself to others and acknowledge that you are here for a distinct purpose, you will discover astonishing freedom from the constant pressure of attempting to be like someone else. You don't have to be the best at everything or live up to some impossible standard. You are enough, just as you are.

I understand it's hard to feel that way, especially when you look around and see other people succeeding in areas where you might struggle. But don't let that make you dissatisfied with your gifts. You may not even be fully aware of all your gifts and talents at this point in your life. Sometimes, it takes time and a bit of faith, but those gifts are there, waiting to be discovered and developed.

When we stop looking sideways at others and start focusing on our unique path, that's when we uncover our true potential. God has given you gifts that are just as valuable as anyone else's—you have to take the time to see them for what they are.

Personal Connections

While this concept works in a small group setting, I've discovered that sharing it with individuals one-on-one maximizes its power. There's something about sitting down with just one individual that allows for a deeper, more personal connection. It creates a safe space where they can open up and feel seen and heard—without the pressure of others.

In those intimate moments, the message isn't just another lesson to learn; it becomes a conversation, a heart-to-heart where the individual can process the meaning of being uniquely made and find genuine hope in that truth. For me, those are the moments where change happens, when someone believes in their value in a way they never have before.

The following example is from a time when I shared this concept with a youth group. Even with almost sixty kids, the impact on them individually was noticeable. They asked well-thought-out questions and had honest reactions to the subject. You could see the teenagers realizing the connection between their unique talents and the freedom not to compare themselves to others.

The LifeWalk Presentation

I begin the LifeWalk—a visual and interactive way to represent the opportunities in a lifetime. I have found duct tape works best. Just remember to fold over one corner to make it easier to pull up. Also, use a contractor's wheel to measure with. The best location is on a street with a slight rise. If you can, set it up so the tapes you place through the high school part are before the crest. They will be totally out of sight from the end. It will all make sense soon. This visual tool makes the reality of life's length and meaning more tangible to whoever I'm working with.[1]

1. Date of birth:
   If working with just one person, have them write their name and date of birth on a strip of duct tape, then place it on the pavement. It marks the starting point. For group presentations, adjust this a bit. Instead of using individual names, have someone write the year they were born on the tape and place it on the street or ground for everyone to see. It serves as a reminder of how far they've come on their journey.

2. Current age:
   Next, use the measuring wheel to map out the number of years they've already lived. Each foot represents one year. If it's a one-on-one session, measure one foot for each year to the person's current age and have them write their age and grade. They will identify with it as you go through the rest. In a group setting, mark out distances from the starting line for each class year: ninth graders at fourteen feet, sophomores at fifteen feet, juniors at sixteen feet, and seniors at seventeen feet. You can also include middle school class identifications. It helps everyone see where they are on the timeline.

3. Year of graduation from high school:
   From the beginning, measure out to eighteen feet and place a piece of duct tape labeled "Graduation." The kids should always be the ones to write on the tape and put it on the pavement. For many teens, graduation seems distant. This puts it in perspective and helps them see how close it is. It gives them a visual of the transition from adolescence to adulthood and the significance of reaching that milestone.

---

1. The suggested LifeWalk distance table is provided in the appendix. See also beyondthesirens.net.

4. Life expectancy is eighty-eight years:
   Now, from the tape labeled "Graduation," measure another seventy feet, bringing us to the life expectancy. I mark this point as the "End of Watch." I explain that firefighters, law enforcement officers, and first responders honor someone who dies in the line of duty with an end-of-watch announcement. They announce their name and badge number by paging it three times and then declare their death as End of Watch.

This is a decisive moment in the presentation, as it visually represents the average span of a person's life. It shows how much life there is to live after high school. Too often, young people can't see past their current struggles. But seeing the seventy feet still ahead changes their perception. It helps them realize that life is a journey with so much more to come, even if things seem overwhelming.

With everyone standing at the eighty-eight-year marker and facing away from the start, ask them to turn and face the starting point. Standing at the tape that represents their life expectancy, make some observations.

Is it difficult to see your middle or high school years from this point? It would not be visible if you used a rise in the street at the beginning. Do those years seem smaller compared to the vast stretch of life that comes after them?

Pause to receive acknowledgment, whether it's a nod or a look of agreement from the group. They should take a moment to take in the distance from the start.

Continue to reinforce the idea:

Think about this: How significant are those middle and high school years compared to the rest of your life? I understand they feel huge right now like everything is riding on what happens during these next few weeks and months, but from here, you can see that they are just a tiny part of a much bigger picture.

Challenge them to do some research on their own:

If you ever get the chance, ask someone who graduated just a couple of years ago, "Do you feel that what you experienced in high school has had any lasting impact on your life now?" I guarantee that most of them will tell you that while they were in high school, it was the most significant part of their identity. However, after they graduated, it rarely had any effect on their life.

This exercise helps them realize that the struggles they're going through now, while they may feel all-consuming, are just the beginning of a much longer story. There's so much more ahead, and the pressure they feel in high school will expire once they graduate.

Next, take the group back along the timeline, measuring off additional significant life milestones:

- Move back twenty-three feet and place a marker labeled "Retirement" age sixty-five. Encourage the kids to come up with the different milestones.
- Then, measure ten more feet toward the start and put down a strip of duct tape labeled "Grandkids" age fifty-five.
- Return another twenty-five feet to mark "Having Kids" at age thirty.
- Go back five feet and add the marker for "Marriage" at age twenty-five.

With the milestones laid out, please return to the spot representing where they are now in high school or middle school. Pause and make this observation.

"From where we stood before, near the End of Watch, could you see these years? They seemed so small, just a sliver in the grand scheme of your life. But standing here, at this moment in time, this is all you can see. They are everything but only because they represent your experiences until now."

Takeaway Two

Introduce suicide concerns:
Think about where you are right now, then look ahead toward the future we just marked out. Do you understand now why we refer to teen suicide as a "permanent solution to a temporary problem?"

Give them a moment to let this settle in. Then, repeat it. You can continue with an example many may remember. In our area, it was this:

Some of you may recall the tragedy of the Marysville-Pilchuck High School shooting. It was a devastating moment in our northwest community—an example of a "permanent solution to a temporary problem." The young man had just broken up with his girlfriend a few days before. Experiencing the overwhelming pain of that moment, he made a choice that would change countless lives forever. It is likely that if he had just waited a couple more days, he would have gotten beyond the immediate pain, and the outcome would have been different.

The point here is to show that the pain they feel right now isn't the whole story. It's a chapter, only part of the book. Life has many more chapters, experiences, and chances for adventures.

The Harsh Realities of Suicide

At this point, explain that you wish to share essential and sobering facts about suicide—things they may not have realized, but that are crucial to understanding the full impact. You would learn and experience these things if you were a first responder on any suicide call.

- The risk of another family member taking their own life is three times higher: once one family member dies by suicide, the ripple effect it creates increases the risk for others in that family. The chaplain who created this presentation was called to the same house three times for the suicide of a different member of the same family. Imagine the heartbreak of returning to the same home, not once but three times, because another family member felt there was no way out. Unfortunately, it isn't just an isolated case.
- Parents, siblings, and close friends never get over it: no matter how much time passes, the pain never entirely fades. The grief of losing someone to suicide leaves a mark that stays with those left behind for the rest of their lives.
- It's not uncommon for parents to leave their circle of friends and their church: parents who lose a child to suicide often feel like they can no longer relate to the people they once called friends. The weight of the loss can lead them to leave long-standing relationships, even changing churches or moving to another location to escape the constant reminder of their pain.
- Many victims of suicide—the family and friends left behind—silently carry their anguish: they feel isolated, believing that no one can understand the depth of their pain. Many feel it's unsafe to seek help because they don't think anyone will truly comprehend what they're going through.

- Parents often blame each other: the grief and shock of losing a child can tear marriages and families apart. Some marriages don't survive the strain that follows a suicide.
- A common question you would hear on a scene: why do they hate me so much to do this to me?
- Guilt: anyone close to the person will blame themselves for missing signs. Friends, siblings, parents, and anyone close to the person who took their life will ask themselves, "Why didn't I see it? Why didn't I do something?"
- Friends of the family often avoid them because they don't know how to act or what to say: it's not that they don't care; they feel helpless. The discomfort of not knowing what to say causes them to drift away when the family needs support the most.
- There's always regret—always the feeling of wishing for one last conversation, a chance to say goodbye.
- The rate of teens attempting to take their own lives is rapidly increasing. It is a problem that isn't going to go away. It's growing. More and more young people are reaching the point where they feel suicide is their only option.

And these are just a few of the consequences. The impact of one person's suicide ripples far beyond what many of us can imagine, affecting family, friends, and entire communities. It leaves behind a trail of broken hearts, shattered lives, unspoken pain, and guilt for not intervening.

Suicide is permanent.

Once you take that step, there's no going back. No second chances. No opportunity to undo it. It's a decision that affects everyone you love in ways you can not imagine—and there's no cure for the pain.

Before you make that choice, please talk to someone. It might feel like no one will understand or like your pain is too much to bear, but some people want to help and will listen. You are not alone, even if it feels that way.

Your life matters. You still have more to add to your story. Take the chance to reach out, and let someone help you through the darkness. Because once you're gone, that's it. The people who love you carry that loss and guilt forever.

Move to the "Graduation" marker. Standing at this spot they will experience both how close they are to graduation and also see that the number of years ahead of them overshadow the next two or three years.

Takeaway Three

Theirs is a quote that has brought comfort and clarity to many people, including myself. The chaplain who created this presentation responded to over a thousand calls where someone had died. He experienced lives cut short, from newborns just a day old to those who lived past one hundred. Those were a reminder that death doesn't play by any rules. Those experiences have taught us just how fragile and temporary life is.

If there's one thing we have learned, it's this: we never have a guarantee for tomorrow. We live as if we have all the time in the world, but none of us knows what the next day will bring.

This brings me to the quote that might sound familiar. It has stayed with me over the years. I first heard it from an unexpected place—the first *Kung Fu Panda* movie. It was not until later that I discovered it came from Eleanor Roosevelt. But despite its simplicity, its message is profound:

Yesterday is history,

Tomorrow is a mystery,

But today is a gift—that's why they call it the present.

Think about that for a moment. Yesterday is gone—it's already written, you can do nothing to change it. Tomorrow hasn't happened yet, and we do not know what it will hold. The only thing we truly have is this moment, this day. We have been given the gift of this moment, this day, and it is entirely up to us how we choose to use it.

Life can sometimes feel overwhelming for everyone, especially when we're caught up in the pain of the past or the uncertainty of the future. But when we realize that the present is all we have, it gives us the freedom to focus on what we can do today—how to make a difference, take one more step forward, and hold on for a little longer.

That's the beauty of life. It's fragile, but it's also precious. And the gift of today is something none of us should take for granted.

Takeaway Four

Were you aware that being bullied or having experienced bullying in the past can give you some significant advantages in life? Does that surprise you or even seem possible right now? Think about it. Here are a few of those advantages:

Advantages of being bullied

1. You learn how to minimize the effects: yes, it still hurts, but you develop ways to cope and protect your heart and mind over time. These skills will make you stronger and will be helpful throughout your life.
2. You tend to listen more than you speak: bullying sometimes forces a person into a quieter, more observant role. While this may seem a disadvantage initially, it may give you a decisive edge. You learn to be thoughtful and listen before you speak, an ability many struggle with.
3. You'll develop the ability to read body language earlier: once you've been the target of bullying, you learn to pick up on non-verbal cues that others miss. This heightened awareness can serve you well in countless situations throughout your life, both personally and professionally.
4. You may carry more compassion and empathy throughout your life: having faced adversity, you will understand the pain others go through. It might allow you to connect more deeply with some people, showing empathy in ways that those who haven't experienced hardship can't.
5. Your relationships could be more profound: because of your experiences, you'll value authentic relationships more than superficial ones. You'll surround yourself with people who genuinely care about you, and those connections will be more meaningful.
6. People will value your input: since you listen carefully and don't rush to judgment, others will seek your perspective. They could see you as thoughtful, someone who can offer insight without jumping to conclusions.
7. You'll have better problem-solving skills: dealing with bullies forces you to find solutions in challenging situations. This ability to navigate

complex emotions and scenarios will make you a more resilient and effective problem solver as you grow.

8. You'll develop more vital social skills to handle stressful situations: facing difficult people early on teaches you how to manage stress and navigate conflict. It can serve you well in high-pressure situations later in life, whether at work or in personal relationships.

9. You'll focus more on problem solving than blaming others: instead of pointing fingers, you'll develop a mindset that seeks solutions. This approach will help you in every aspect of life, making you a more constructive person.

Advantages of being a bully: ask for their help coming up with items. You can have these for backup.

1. They think they are popular: bullies may think they're on top of the world, but their sense of popularity is often fleeting and shallow.
2. They might impress others temporarily: yes, bullies may gain temporary attention or control, but that power is often short lived and based on fear, not respect.
3. They might avoid being bullied themselves: by intimidating others, bullies might prevent becoming targets themselves, but this only reinforces their cycle of aggression.
4. There may be more, but I need help to think of any right now.

Disadvantages of being a bully: first, ask them to come up with their own.

1. Those who they constantly try to impress are always on edge, hoping they won't become the next target: friendships formed out of fear aren't stable. These "friends" often try to avoid becoming the next victim.
2. People know bullies tear others down to build themselves up: deep down, their peers recognize the insecurity that fuels the bullying. It can undermine any genuine respect or admiration they might seek.

3. There's a fundamental lack of trust in bullies: people may associate with them, but they don't trust them. People often perceive bullies as unpredictable and dangerous.
4. Their relationships are shallower: instead of forming deep connections, bullies create relationships based on power dynamics and manipulation. They limit their appeal to building genuine friendships.
5. They are self-centered: bullies often focus only on their own needs and desires, pushing others away. This self-centeredness makes it hard for them to sustain meaningful relationships.
6. They blame others for their problems: bullies avoid taking responsibility for their actions. Instead, they deflect blame onto others, which prevents them from growing emotionally or learning from their mistakes.
7. Their school friendships drift away after graduation: once they leave the controlled environment of school, bullies often lose their power and influence, and their friends move on, leaving them isolated.

Conclusion

- I hope you've gained a new perspective on life, challenges, and yourself. We've covered much ground today, and I want to leave you with a few final thoughts.
- You have a unique identity and a purpose only you can fulfill. The struggles you're facing in school, stress, self-doubt, or bullying are part of the journey but are temporary. High school is the center of your world now, but when you step back and see the bigger picture, you'll realize these moments won't define you.
- Don't compare yourself to others. You have gifts and strengths that no one else does. You are here for a reason; there is so much more ahead than you can see now.
- Please reach out if you ever feel like there's no way out. Talk to someone. It might seem like no one understands, but people care deeply about you. Suicide is a permanent response to a temporary problem, and I promise you—there is a future beyond the pain you're feeling today.

- The ripple effects of suicide are real. It impacts everyone—family, friends, even entire communities. The pain doesn't go away. That's why it's crucial to hold on, reach out, and remember that hope exists, even in the darkest moments.
- And always remember: Yesterday is history, tomorrow is a mystery, but today is a gift—that's why we call it the present. Every day, you have the gift of life.
- Embrace who you are, face challenges, and know that your life matters. The world is a better place with you in it.

Thank them for their attention and questions. Always ask if anyone would like to talk to you privately, and that it would be an honor.

Appendix

How Children Grieve

GRIEVING IS A DEEPLY personal and intricate process, but for children it displays differently than it does in adults. Children have unique thoughts and emotional cycles making their grief expressions and coping mechanisms distinct from those of grown-ups. This section delves into the nuances of how children mourn, aiming to shed light on their often-overlooked pain, and provide a roadmap for those supporting them.

At the core, children, like adults, feel the pain of loss deeply. However, their understanding and articulation of that pain vary based on their developmental stage. A toddler may not understand death's permanence and could ask when the deceased will return. Teenagers might grapple with experiential questions while also facing the tumult of adolescence.

1. Grieving based on Developmental Stages:

   - Infants and Toddlers (0–2 years old): They might not understand the concept of death, but they sense when a caregiver is absent. Their grief might manifest as fussiness, changes in sleeping and eating habits, or general irritability.

   - Preschoolers (3–5 years old): Children often think in literal terms at this age. They might believe that death is reversible, likening it to sleep. Behavioral regressions, such as bed-wetting or thumb-sucking, can be grief reactions.

   - Elementary School Age (6–12 years old): Children in this group grasp the finality of death but might not understand its universality or causality. They might feel guilt, thinking they somehow caused the death. Curiosity about death is also common, and they might ask detailed questions.

- Adolescents (13–18 years old): Teenagers often react to death like adults. However, their developmental quest for independence can complicate their grieving process. They might oscillate between wanting to be alone and desiring connection or support.

2. The Oscillation of Grief:

It's crucial to understand that children might not continuously exhibit their grief. They can oscillate between grieving moments and regular play or school activities. This intermittent grieving can puzzle adults but is a natural protective mechanism for children, giving them breaks from the intensity of their emotions.

3. Expressions of Grief:

Children might express their grief through play, art, or stories. It's common to see themes of death, loss, or reunions in their creative expressions. It is their way of processing and making sense of their feelings.

4. The Role of Questions:

Children are naturally curious, and their questions about death can sometimes be unexpected. They might ask about the specifics of death, the aftermath, or related rituals like funerals. Answering these questions honestly, in age-appropriate ways, can give them a sense of security and understanding.

5. The Importance of Routine:

Routine can offer solace. The predictability of daily life can become a pillar of support for a grieving child. Maintaining routines, even amidst the chaos of loss, can be beneficial.

In conclusion, recognizing and understanding how children grieve is pivotal in supporting them through one of life's toughest challenges. Their resilience is immense, but the guidance and support of understanding adults can make a world of difference. Remember the foundational knowledge that children, in their ways, are trying to navigate the turbulent waters of

grief just like the rest of us.

Navajo Way of Listening

THE NAVAJO WAY OF listening, often rooted in Navajo culture and spirituality, is profoundly reflective and attentive. While I cannot capture every nuance of the Navajo culture, here's a general description:

- Deep respect and presence: The Navajo way of listening emphasizes total presence and deep respect. When someone is speaking, the listener is not merely hearing the words but is also absorbing the emotions, intentions, and spiritual essence behind the words.
- Patience: Traditional Navajo communication values taking one's time. There's no rush. In traditional Navajo communication, individuals incorporate silences into conversations and do not perceive them as awkward pauses but as essential moments of reflection and processing.
- Holistic listening: Navajo listening isn't just about the ears. It involves the whole being. It's about observing body language, noting the tone of voice, and feeling the energy or emotion behind the words. This holistic approach ensures a deep understanding and connection between the speaker and the listener.
- Spiritual connection: For the Navajo, communication is not just routine. It's deeply spiritual. Words have power, and listening is a way of honoring the sacredness of the individual and the message they convey.
- Contextual understanding: The Navajo approach to listening also considers the broader context. Listeners may consider the environment, historical and familial backgrounds, and other external factors that might influence the speaker's message.

- Absence of interruption: It is impolite to interrupt someone while they're speaking. Even if there's disagreement or a different perspective, the listener waits patiently for their turn to share.
- Storytelling: This is the primary method through which the Navajo people transmit their teaching and wisdom. Thus, listening becomes an essential skill from a young age, as stories often convey lessons, histories, and moral values.

In a world dominated by quick exchanges and fleeting attention spans, the Navajo way of listening is a profound reminder of the power and importance of truly being present and connecting deeply with others. It's a practice that fosters understanding, empathy, and connection at a level that many modern cultures might find unfamiliar but incredibly enriching.

LifeWalk Progression Table

Distances and Labels

Distance	Label	Side Notes / Talking Points
Starting Point	Date of Birth	Have participants write their names on the starting strip.
Your Current Age	Present Grade	Example: If their age is 14, walk 14 feet.
18 Feet	Graduating High School	This is an average graduation age.
22 Feet	Graduating College	Based on a four-year degree.
88 Feet	Expected Life Span	Based on averages.
Return to Present		Encourage participants to reflect. "We will now fill in some other milestones."

Additional Milestones

Distance	Label	Side Notes / Talking Points
Your Current Age	Present Grade	Highlight how short the distance is until leaving high school. Challenge participants: "Ask someone who graduated if high school had a lasting impact."
14 Feet	Brain is full size	Brain's wiring continues to reorganize into early adulthood, making teens highly influenced by their environment.
18 Feet	High School Graduation	It is a pivotal milestone for many.
19 Feet	Red Marker: 10–19	Use a red Sharpie; don't explain it yet.
22 Feet	College Graduation	Another pivotal milestone.

Distance	Label	Side Notes / Talking Points
25 Feet	Brain maturity	The brain reaches maturity, though changes continue. Executive functions like planning are fully developed.
25–32 Feet	Finding a partner / marriage	Point out: "Another key milestone often happens around age 25."
30 Feet	First child	Median age for first childbirth. Discuss new joys and responsibilities.
60 Feet	First grandchild	"Grandkids are more fun than kids—you can spoil them and send them home."
62 Feet	Retirement	The average age of retirement in the US.
88 Feet	Life expectancy	Reflect on how much life remains ahead.

Return to red marker: Ages 10–19

Side Notes / Talking Points

More than 20 percent of teens have seriously considered suicide.

Suicide is the second-leading cause of death among teenagers.

Suicide is a permanent solution to a temporary problem. From here, you can see hope.

Impact: At least six people will experience life-changing consequences if someone takes their own life.

Challenge: "If you're feeling this way, talk to someone. You're not alone."

Family Impact: Siblings are three times more likely to consider suicide if a brother or sister takes their own life. I have been to the same home for three different suicide calls.

www.ingramcontent.com/pod-product-compliance
Lightning Source LLC
Chambersburg PA
CBHW071204160426
43196CB00011B/2192